Saints and Angels All Around

Saints and Angels All Around

Gregory J. Wismar

SAINT LOUIS

The number of books on the subject of saints and angels is
historically large and today is constantly expanding.
Quotes attributed to the saints in this volume come from a variety of
sources. Of interest might be the following volumes, which could be
consulted for more perspectives on the saints or angles included in
this book, as well as for information on other saints and angels.
Among the many books available for further study are
The Penguin Dictionary of Saints, edited by Donald Attwater;
A Calendar of Saints by James Bentley; *A Book of Angels*
by Sophy Burnham; *Saints for All Seasons,* edited by John Delaney;
Saints Alive! by Anne Fremantle; *Angels: an Endangered Species*
by Malcom Godwin; *101 Saints* by David Liptak; *Lives of Saints* by
Thomas Plassmann; *The Fathers of the Eastern Church* and *The Fathers
of the Western Church* by Robert Payne; and *Butler's Lives of the Saints,*
edited by Herbert Thurston. There are numerous volumes beyond
this list that can be found in both religious and secular bookstores, as
well as in local libraries.

Copyright © 1996 Concordia Publishing House
3558 S. Jefferson Avenue, St. Louis, MO 63118-3968
Manufactured in the United States of America

Library of Congress Cataloging-in-Publication Data
Wismar, Gregory J., 1946–
    Saints and angels all around / Gregory J. Wismar.
        p.   cm.
    ISBN 0-570-04816-8
    1. Christian saints—Meditations. 2. Christian saints—Biogra-
phy. 3. Angels—Meditations. I. Title. II. Series.
BR1710.W57   1995
270`.092`2—dc20   95-9655
[B]

1 2 3 4 5 6 7 8 9 10   05 04 03 02 01 00 99 98 97 96

This book is gratefully dedicated
to the saints in my family and to all the saints
of the congregations where it has been
my joy to serve: Immanuel, St. Paul's,
Redeemer, Messiah, and Christ the King

Contents

Elizabeth	54
Francis of Assisi	57
Gabriel	60
Gregory	63
Helena	66
Hilary	69
Hilda	72
Hippolytus	75
Ignatius	78
Jerome	81
John Chrysostom	84
Justin Martyr	87
Katherine	90
Laurence	93
Margaret	96
Martin	99
Michael	102

I sing a song to the saints of God,
    patient and brave and true,
    who toiled and fought and lived and died
    for the Lord they loved and knew.
And one was a doctor, and one was a queen,
    and one was a shepherdess on the green:
they were all of them saints of God—
    and I mean, God helping, to be one too.

They loved their Lord so dear, so dear,
    and his love made them strong;
    and they followed the right, for Jesus' sake,
    the whole of their good lives long.
And one was a soldier, and one was a priest,
    and one was slain by a fierce wild beast:
and there's not any reason—no, not the least,
    why I shouldn't be one too.

They lived not only in ages past,
    there are hundreds of thousands still,
    the world is bright with the joyous saints
    who love to do Jesus' will.
You can meet them in school, or in lanes, or at sea,
    in church, or in trains, or in shops, or at tea,
for the saints of God are just folk like me,
    and I mean to be one too.

—Lesbia Scott (b. 1898)

Preface

A Few Words about Saints and Angels

People who are like us and beings who aren't: welcome to the fascinating world of saints and angels! Whether we realize it or not, saints and angels are all around us—angels by their presence and saints by memories passed along generation to generation. Getting to know saints and angels better can encourage us in our faith and inform our lives. The devotions in this book take a quick look at a cross-section of saints from the first 14 centuries of the Christian church and at four angels. Their experiences can help us find inspiration for our times as well as guide us to a new closeness to their Lord and ours. They are excellent Christian company for us!

The names of some saints might be new to you: Hippolytus, Chrysostom, and Radegund, for example. The names of others, however, are not strange to us. We see their names around us in cities and towns, such as Saint Augustine, Florida, and Saint Ansgar, Iowa, and in church names such as Saint Ambrose and Saint Thomas Aquinas. In the past, some parents named their children for specific saints (for example, Bridget and Patrick) to afford the children special blessing and protection. Through the centuries, saints' days have called for notable observances and special activities such as processionals and parades. But what do we know of the saints besides their names? Why set them apart? And what can they teach us today?

As you read these hagiographies (the technical term for stories about saints' lives), you will discover people like yourself who offered outstanding service to God. The 36 saints in this volume are representative of women and men from a variety of nations over an extended period of time. Each is interesting and worthy of far more discovery than this guide is able to supply. One of the purposes of this book is to give a "jump start" that may motivate you to discover more about these and other saints and angels.

Almost 500 years ago Martin Luther voiced his opinion that "next to Holy Scripture there certainly is no more useful book for Christendom than that of the lives of the saints." They deserve our honor, for in their lives God showed examples of his mercy and taught generations of believers. We honor their memory—and particularly God himself—when we imitate their faith and other virtues.

Getting to know some saints by name, place, and date will help you to "rub shoulders" with them, to discover how they faithfully and purposefully lived out a span of years in a certain corner of the earth. The information in the appendix will help you put names and dates and times together in sequence and order. Please refer to it often as you travel through the centuries represented on these pages.

Although saints are in the majority in this volume, the book is also about angels. (The Bible names two: Gabriel and Michael. Other literature from biblical times names two others: Raphael and Uriel.) In recent years angels have again become very popular. A recent Gallup Poll notes that more than three teens in four now say they believe in angels. People, young and old and in-between, are curious about these messengers from God, often pictured in works of art as having wings and halos. Like the saints, angels have fallen in and out of favor over the centuries. The first years of the Christian era saw discussion and even disagreement about the role of angels. Saint Paul had to mention in one of his letters that Christians are not to worship angels (Colossians 2:18). At the time of the Reformation, Luther felt it necessary to remind Christians that angels are real. "It is certain that they are waiting for our coming into our future fatherland but also that they are truly around us in this life, providing for and guiding our affairs, if we would only firmly believe it." The question today, though, seems to be what they are like and what they do. Many "New Age" books go far beyond biblical truth. The reality is that these magnificent beings serve God and his will, not the whims of humanity. Therefore, meeting the angels (and the saints) is appropriate for every age.

In the Bible, the number 40 often stands for completion. In this volume, we will meet 40 saints and angels through portions of Scripture and historical commentary. Each devotional section concludes with a prayer thought. Birth and death dates, some noted as approximate (c.), will help frame the lifetime of each saint. (Angels need no such notation.)

May our gracious Lord, who is praised
by saints and angels all around, bless your reflection,
your learning, and your living to his glory.

Saint Ambrose
(340–397)

In the Right Place at the Right Time

If anyone sets his heart on being an overseer [a bishop], he desires a noble task. 1 Timothy 3:1

God has a way of finding the right person for the right job at the right time, and sometimes he does it in unexpected and surprising ways. Ambrose was one of those right people, but he didn't know it—at least not right away.

As a child, Ambrose proudly announced one time, "I shall one day be bishop!" That title, "Bishop," stuck to him as his nickname, even though his studies and career choice took him in another direction. He entered the Roman civil service, as had his father before him. Quickly he gained a reputation for fairness and hard work. Before long he became governor in northern Italy, ruling from the city of Milan.

When the local bishop of that region died, conflict broke out in Milan between two possible successors. When a crowd gathered in the city center,

Ambrose, as governor, went to keep order. While he was speaking, a child called out his name and his nickname: "Ambrose-Bishop! Ambrose-Bishop!" The crowd echoed the words, and the new Bishop of Milan was chosen by acclamation. Although the choice seemed unplanned, God had found the right person for the right job at the right time.

In every way, Ambrose was a bishop to his people. Working tirelessly for the church, he gave it all of his personal wealth and the best of his creative efforts. He faithfully served as bishop of Milan for almost 23 years, but his influence on the Christian church reached far beyond Italy. Christians today still sing hymns Ambrose wrote, including the great Advent hymn "Savior of the Nations, Come." His work on chanting was one of the first steps in the evolution to today's choral composition. Truly, Ambrose lived up to the vocation to which he had been called.

Life as a bishop was never easy for Ambrose. He dealt with political struggles in the empire, doctrinal controversies in the church, and personal difficulties in his own life. Yet, he did so with confidence and faith. When he was near death he was able to say, "I have not so lived among you as to be ashamed to live on; but I am not afraid to die, for our Lord is good."

In his first epistle, Saint John reminds us of what we have been called. "How great is the love the Father has lavished on us," he writes, "that we should be called children of God! And that is what we are!" (1 John 3:1). Like Ambrose, we have a God to glorify, the gracious

God who has made us members of his immediate family in his Son, Jesus Christ, through whom we are reconciled by his work on the cross.

December 7, the day of Saint Ambrose on the calendar, is an exception to the rule. Most saints are commemorated on their death days, but Ambrose is remembered on the day in 374 when he was named Bishop of Milan.

You know each of your sheep, gracious Shepherd, and you call us by name—your name. We belong to you. Help us always to speak and act like the people we are, children of your Father, that through our witness of faith and life you may be glorified. Amen.

You may also want to pray for church and political leaders and hymn writers.

Saint Anselm
(1033–1109)

For Love of the Church

Now to him who is able to do immeasurably more than all we ask or imagine, according to his power that is at work within us, to him be glory in the church and in Christ Jesus throughout all generations, for ever and ever! Amen. Ephesians 3:20–21

The traditional symbol for Saint Anselm, the ship, reminds us of his travels between Normandy, England, and Italy on behalf of the church he loved. Throughout his entire adult life, he protected the rights of the church from the designing greed of secular rulers in his adopted homeland of England.

Born into an affluent Italian family in 1033, his father wanted Anselm to become a soldier or merchant. However, the son's love for the church took him to northern France, where he became a monk instead. He rose quickly through the authority structure of the church and was appointed abbot of the monastery at Bec in Normandy. Part of his responsibility was to oversee church properties in England. On one of his journeys there, the local people acclaimed him the new archbishop of Canterbury, leader of the English church.

Anselm did not want to become the archbishop. He knew that he would come into direct conflict with King William, who decreed that there would be no new archbishop. Rather, he as king would take over the properties of the church and also would appoint the bishops and abbots—something that church leaders had always done previously. Although Anselm did not want to be archbishop, his love for the church changed his mind. After prayerful thought, he agreed to accept the position, providing the king would back off from his decree. For a while it seemed as if things would work out. Unfortunately, William had a short memory regarding his promises and sought again to take away the church's rights. In disappointment, Anselm left England and went to Rome to gain support for his claims to authority and the church's rights.

While waiting for things to change in England, Anselm found good use for his time in Italy. He wrote a number of books, letters, and treatises linking theology and the things of God with reason and intellectual inquiry. His book *Why God Became Man* soon became a Christian classic.

Anselm's scholarly search came from his faith in Jesus. He wrote, "I long, O God, to know Thee, to love Thee, that I may rejoice in Thee. And if I cannot attain to full joy in this life, may I at least advance from day to day until that joy shall come to me in full." To rejoice in

God is the life goal of every believer in Christ. Anselm had certain hope of reaching that goal, as may we, because Jesus suffered, died, and rose again to forgive all sins and to bring us joy that is greater than any disappointment or sorrow.

Anselm hoped that things would go well for him in England when Henry succeeded William as king. But Henry did not favor church rights either. Anselm kept on traveling and meeting and praying, hoping that the situation would improve. Finally it did. King Henry and Archbishop Anselm agreed on the church's right to appoint the bishops and abbots. They also agreed that church leaders owed homage to the king for protecting their possessions. At last the church in England was at peace and able to bring greater glory to God, thanks to Anselm's efforts. Eventually the archbishop became such a good friend to the king that when the monarch traveled outside of England, he left Anselm in charge.

During Holy Week in the year 1109, the saintly Anselm died at Canterbury. He is remembered on April 21.

Gracious Lord, we thank you for the blessings we receive through the church. Help us honor, support, and cherish it, for we know that Christ loves the church and gave himself for it. We ask this in his holy name. Amen.

You may also want to pray for the church in England.

Saint Ansgar
(801–865)

Looking beyond Disappointments

Who shall separate us from the love of Christ? Shall trouble or hardship or persecution or famine or nakedness or danger or sword? ... No, in all these things we are more than conquerors through him who loved us. Romans 8:35, 37

If people knew about Murphy's Law 1200 years ago, they might well have called it "Ansgar's Law" instead. In Saint Ansgar's life everything that could possibly go wrong seemed to go wrong. Every mission effort he started resulted in failure. Converts came to faith in Christ by the preaching of others; almost nothing resulted from Ansgar's preaching. On more than one occasion he even had to flee from his mission fields to preserve his life. But Ansgar kept on trying and, as a result of his groundwork, many years later the Gospel took root and spread throughout Scandinavia.

Born into a noble French family at the start of the ninth century, Ansgar became a monk with a mission: to bring the lands of northern Europe under the lordship of Christ. His first efforts took him to what is now Denmark and Sweden. At first his preaching, persuasion, and occasional gifts to the local king seemed to bear fruit as he attempted to build churches in these lands. However, his initial success was undone by an invasion of Norsemen in 845. Ansgar was forced to retreat to Bremen, Germany, where he served faithfully, if unremarkably, as bishop. But he did not abandon his northern mission.

About 10 years later he headed back to Jutland (western Denmark), preaching that Jesus Christ changes people. King Erik and his subjects believed this Good News—that through Jesus and his cross we are forgiven and made clean. And the fearsome pattern of slavery that had existed since the start of Viking times began to crumble. However, even these final years of mission work were ultimately undone by a series of pagan invasions.

Ansgar left us an example of patience and kindness. When asked about the importance of being able to perform miracles, he said, "Were God to choose me to do such things, I would ask him for one miracle only— that by his power he would make me a good man." Ansgar's faith helped him look beyond his disappointments. Even when he could not see the results, he took his stand on Jesus' promise: "I tell you the truth, anyone who has faith in me will do what I have been doing. He will do even greater things than these, because I am going to the Father" (John 14:12). It was not until two centuries after his death in 865 that Scandinavia was reestablished as a Christian region. Ansgar, the "Apostle of the North," is remembered on February 3.

Strengthen us when we become discouraged in your service, Lord. Help us persevere, through all our earthly journeys, doing those things that you did. We ask this for your love's sake. Amen.

You may also want to pray for the church in Denmark and Sweden.

Saint Athanasius
(c. 295–373)

Alone against the World

Preach the Word; be prepared in season and out of season; correct, rebuke and encourage—with great patience and careful instruction. 2 Timothy 4:2

Athanasius must have appreciated these words of encouragement that Saint Paul had forwarded to Timothy, for his ministry seemed to be out of season as often as it was in season. While serving as leader of the church at Alexandria, Egypt, for almost half of the fourth century, Athanasius was exiled five different times and almost murdered twice. This happened all because he insisted on teaching what the apostolic church had always taught: that Jesus Christ is true God.

The fourth century brought major change in the church. For the first time, Christianity was legalized and became the dominant religion of the Roman Empire. This new status, however, brought with it unexpected problems. Beginning with Constantine, each Roman emperor took such a personal interest in the church that often its teaching reflected the ideas of whoever was in power at the time. And if an emperor was not an orthodox believer, only the brave or foolhardy would try to defend true apostolic doctrine. At times, heresy flourished.

Athanasius was one such "fool." The emperor at the time followed the teachings of a certain Arius, an Egyptian priest who taught that Jesus was a creation of God and not fully divine, that the Son was neither true God nor eternal. Athanasius was one of the few who spoke out. The title of one of his works, written in exile, tells the story: "Alone against the World."

No matter who was emperor, Athanasius continued to preach and teach Jesus Christ as true God, who came into the world as a man to suffer and die to pay the price of our redemption. Athanasius wrote that Jesus "did not come to make a display of his glory. He came to heal. ... For this is his glory, this the miracle of his divinity, that he changed our sufferings for his happiness. For being life, he died that we may be made alive."

Athanasius was faithfully alive in Jesus. His faith lives on in his writings, which were widely circulated and are still greatly prized. Centuries later, a monk advised, "If you find a book by Athanasius and have no paper on which to copy it, write it on your shirt."

The faith of Saint Athanasius is reflected in the Athanasian Creed, named in his honor, though he did not write it. Traditionally spoken in the church on Trinity Sunday, this creed reflects the faith that Athanasius defended throughout and with his life. It states, in part,

"But the Godhead of the Father, of the Son, and of the Holy Spirit is all one: the glory equal, the majesty coeternal." The last-written of the three major ecumenical creeds, it patiently and carefully confesses the doctrine of the Trinity, which is at the heart of orthodox Christian belief. An example of courageous faith for all times, Athanasius died peacefully in 373, finally restored to his church office at Alexandria. He is remembered in the church on May 2.

Strengthen us, Lord, so that we keep our confession whole and undefiled. Help us to worship the Trinity faithfully and firmly, holding the right faith to the end. In the name of Jesus, our incarnate Savior. Amen.

You may also want to pray that the church will be defended from heresy.

Saint Augustine
(354–430)

The Power of a Bible Passage

Let us behave decently, as in the daytime, not in orgies and drunkenness, not in sexual immorality and debauchery, not in dissension and jealousy. Rather, clothe yourselves with the Lord Jesus Christ, and do not think about how to gratify the desires of the sinful nature. Romans 13:13–14

Scripture is powerful. Saint Augustine read just one passage, the section quoted above from Romans 13, and it changed not only his life but also the direction of the Christian church. Augustine later told about that special encounter with God's Word in an Italian garden on a hot summer afternoon in 386. "It was as though the light of salvation had been poured into my heart," he wrote. The experience led him to quit his career as a teacher of worldly philosophy and rhetoric and to become a forceful Christian leader who kept the whole church on course through troublesome times. His extensive writings helped to shape the church's theology permanently.

Born into an African family, Augustine learned the basic teachings of the Christian faith at home. Although his father was not a believer until shortly before his death, his mother, Monica, devoutly shared her faith in Christ with her son. But as Augustine grew, his mind was set on other things. His early years were filled with the behaviors against which the Romans had been warned by St. Paul. However, neither wild living nor fame, neither success nor wealth brought Augustine the sense of completeness for which he yearned. Days with his books and students, first at Rome and then at Milan, and nights with his mistress and his young son seemed to have an emptiness to them. He was restless, open, and waiting.

It was then that the Holy Spirit began his life-changing work in Augustine. Through his reading of Scripture in that summer garden and following his Baptism by Saint Ambrose, Augustine discovered that God had filled his life with blessing. Finally Augustine was at peace—the same peace God grants us as we live each day in the power of our Baptism; the peace that comes from knowing that God is for us and that his Spirit lives in us.

After making that discovery, Augustine wrote to God, "You have created us for yourself, and our hearts cannot rest until they find repose in you." Giving up his mistress, Augustine returned to Africa and began a new life as a church worker and writer.

Augustine served for 34 years as Bishop of Hippo, a city in North Africa. During that time the church was faced with many heresies and challenges, yet he patiently and precisely addressed each one of them. He constantly reasserted the clear teachings of the Scriptures. Many years later, Martin Luther was profoundly influenced by Augustine in his rediscovery of the doctrine of justification by grace through faith in Christ who paid for our sins.

Augustine also cared passionately about the local people under his spiritual care. He once said, "I do not wish to be saved without you. Why am I in the world? Not only to live in Jesus Christ, but to live in him with you. This is my passion, my honor, my glory, my joy, and my riches." A few verses from the Bible had changed and shaped Augustine, whose legacy of books, letters, and sermons continues to inspire Christian readers. Most frequently read are his famous spiritual works *The City of God* and *Confessions.* Time spent reading Augustine is time well spent. Saint Augustine's day on the calendar of the saints is generally celebrated on August 28. Among his writings is this prayer:

O God, to turn from you is to fall, to turn to you is to rise, and to stand with you is to abide forever. Grant us help in all we do, guidance in all our confusion, protection in all our dangers, and a place in all our sorrows; through Jesus Christ, our Lord. Amen.

You may also want to pray for those who teach in the church and for the church in North Africa.

Saint Basil
(329–379)

"What a Great Person!"

Whoever wants to become great among you must be your servant, and whoever wants to be first must be slave of all. Mark 10:43

"What a great person!" Perhaps you have said that about someone at some time or other. The Eastern Church, which includes most of Christianity east of the center of the Mediterranean Sea (in countries such as Russia, Syria, Lebanon, Greece, and Albania), officially has called Basil "the Great." By his family associations and by his life, Basil merited his "great" name.

Basil was born into a "great" family early in the fourth century. His father and mother, a sister, two brothers, and even his grandmother, Macrina, are listed on the official calendar of saints. Their home in Caesarea of Cappadocia (part of Asia Minor) was alive with Christian conversation and activity.

The Christian church itself, however, was plagued with doctrinal controversy. It took leaders of great courage and determination to maintain an orthodox confession of faith when even the Roman emperor was following Arianism, a popular heresy of the time, which denied that Jesus was fully divine as well as truly human. (See "Saint Athanasius.")

Basil, elected archbishop of his hometown of Caesarea in 370, held firm to the faith pronounced at the Council of Nicaea some 45 years before, the faith that we express in the Nicene Creed. As we do today, the people under his spiritual care could confess that Jesus Christ is "begotten, not made, being of one substance with the Father, by whom all things were made." It is Jesus our Lord, true God from eternity, who saved us and it is he whom we worship. The Good News of the Gospel—that, in person, God came to earth to fulfill the Law perfectly for us and to die on the cross for the forgiveness of our sins—is what Basil proclaimed in word and reflected in great deeds of Christian service.

Although he frequently associated with world and church leaders, Basil kept his own life simple and humble. In order to encourage those virtues in others, he founded the first Christian community for men. His sister, also named Macrina, established one like it for women. Basil's rules for monastery life, still observed today throughout the lands of the Eastern Church, detail how people who voluntarily form a community of brothers or sisters in the faith should behave individually and together.

Tirelessly assisting the poor, caring for the sick, and working for the betterment of his home city, Basil neglected his health and died at the age of 49 on New Year's Day in 379. Basil, a great servant of Christ, is remembered by the Eastern Church on January 1; other Christians commemorate him on January 2 or on June 14, along with his brother, Gregory of Nyssa, and his friend Gregory of Nazianzus.

It is greatness in faith that we ask from you, O Lord. Lead us in ways that are pleasing to you, and fill us with your Spirit that we may strive to walk in the faith of the great saints. This we ask through Jesus Christ, who with you and the Holy Spirit are one God forever. Amen.

You may also want to pray for pastors and the poor.

Saint Benedict
(480–543)

Keeping a Light in a Dark Age

Everything should be done in a fitting and orderly way.
1 Corinthians 14:40

Heroes don't always carry weapons or ride white horses into battle. Some notable saints have won crucial victories and accomplished lasting good in peaceable, quiet ways. Benedict won an important victory for the Christian faith and for all of Western civilization by organizing religious communities during a turbulent time in Europe. A hero of his era, he patiently gave structure to the monastic movement established earlier by Saint Basil and others, setting rules by which men and women lived together as Christian brothers and sisters in an ordered and productive way.

The monasteries themselves were not the major contribution. Rather, it was the work they did. Through the monasteries he established, skills like bookbinding, painting, and stained-glass making were saved during the darkest times of the Dark Ages, when savage invasions and wars dominated people's lives. In Benedict's harmonious religious houses, music, art, and literature were preserved, treasured, and developed, and the Graeco-Roman cultural heritage was kept alive.

Benedict, the father of Western monasticism, was born in Italy in 480, just four years after the fall of the city of Rome to invading northern tribes. As he grew up, daily life seemed unstable and the world was chaotic. Like young men and women of different centuries (including our own), Benedict chose to remove himself from the society he saw collapsing around him. However, instead of escaping his world through drunkenness or the sensual excesses of the decaying Roman culture, Benedict hid out in a cave and devoted himself to prayer and meditation. Soon his reputation for Christian holiness of life became well known throughout Italy. Searching pilgrims found their way to his cave, looking for some kind of structure for their lives in a chaotic society. The right man at the right time, Benedict offered people of all ages and backgrounds a new and orderly way for a Christian communal life, one that visibly expressed being in the world but not of the world.

Blending Roman law with Christian tradition and mixing in a good measure of common sense, Benedict established what came to be known as the "Holy Rule" for monks. Its 73 chapters outlined a life of stability that included a strict daily routine, mannerly living, and obedience to those in authority. Observing that "idleness is the enemy of the soul," Benedict made sure that the brothers and sisters in his religious communities would work as well as pray and study.

Benedict's example of balancing work with worship and action with reflection is a model for each of us to follow in our own daily lives. A special feature of his rule was its emphasis on Christian hospitality. Rule 3 states, "All guests who come to a monastery shall be received as though they were Christ." By welcoming strangers and preserving learning, the Benedictine monasteries held together the cultural fabric of Europe through challenging times. Benedict's rule became a blessing to the Middle Ages and provided a legacy that benefits us still today as we put our Christian lives in order. Benedict's day on the calendar of the church is usually celebrated on March 21.

Lord of time and eternity, we thank you for the men and women who enlightened the darkness of their centuries with the light of the Gospel—the news of your great love for us in Christ who died for us. Help us to be dedicated, patient, and hospitable in our times, a blessing to many, including those who follow after us. In Jesus' name. Amen.

You may also want to pray for the courage to put Christ first in all things.

Saint Bernard
(1090–1153)

Busy, Busy, Busy

Humble yourselves, therefore, under God's mighty hand, that he may lift you up in due time. Cast all your anxiety on him because he cares for you. 1 Peter 5:6–7

Being named "Man of the Year" or "Woman of the Decade" is a great honor. Bernard of Clairvaux, the dominant figure in Europe in the 1100s, has often been called the "Man of the 12th Century." Martin Luther considered him "the greatest monk that ever lived." Indeed, Bernard was a great monk—and much more.

Born into a noble French family in 1090, Bernard could have chosen the life of a powerful lord, a gallant soldier, or a wealthy landowner. Instead, at age 22, he persuaded a group of his brothers and friends to enter a monastery with him to begin lives of devotion, work, and prayer. Bernard excelled as a monk and soon was given charge of a monastery of his own at Clairvaux, which became the "mother house" of some 68 other abbeys located throughout Europe.

Life in a monastery was anything but comfortable by our standards. The brothers lived in unheated cells and ate coarse and simple food. Much of their day was spent in contemplation, hard manual labor, or painstaking copying of manuscripts. In addition to his regular duties, Bernard also wrote letters, sermons, and hymns, including "O Sacred Head, Now Wounded" and "O Jesus, King Most Wonderful," both Christian classics.

Throughout his life, Bernard stayed close to the Scriptures and the Lord Jesus proclaimed in its pages. He explained that he used the Bible in his preaching, "not so much in order to expound the words as to reach people's hearts." Through all of his sermons he proclaimed that Jesus is the true friend and deliverer of sinners. As a preacher, Bernard fearlessly spoke difficult and challenging messages because they were God's truth. The hundreds of manuscripts he left behind show that he was willing to preach "in season and out of season" (2 Timothy 4:2).

Bernard combined contemplation with boundless activity across Europe. He settled disputes over who should be kings and popes, how clergy should live, and how Christian lands should deal with threats from invading Muslim warriors. He dealt with both heresies and disasters, including the results of the ill-fated Second Crusade. No wonder that one of his traditional symbols is the beehive like St. Ambrose.

The older he became, the more Bernard was called on as a mediator. In 1153 he successfully worked out a truce between two rival areas in France, but it cost him his health. Shortly after returning to Clairvaux that summer, he died, surrounded by people whose lives he had shaped and blessed. His day on the church calendar is August 20.

Help us to find greatness in service, Lord. Whatever songs we have in our lives, help us sing them in your praise. Whatever words we speak, help us use them to build up others. Let our busyness always be about your business. In Jesus' name we pray. Amen.

You may also want to pray for a greater love for Christ.

Saint Boniface
(c. 673–c. 754)

The Blessed Wood-Chopper

They will be called oaks of righteousness, a planting of the LORD for the display of his splendor. Isaiah 61:3

An oak tree and an ax traditionally symbolize Saint Boniface, known as the apostle to the Germans. He stands tall among the church leaders of the Middle Ages because of his exceptional teaching ability, his valuable organizational skills, and his untiring missionary spirit.

Winfrid (his given name) was born in Crediton, England, to a family that recently had emigrated from Saxony (central Germany). Though educated from the age of seven in English monastery schools, he grew up with a special spiritual concern for people back on the European continent who still followed pagan ways. That concern turned into action when Winfrid, then 40 years old, and some fellow monks went to preach the Gospel in Friesland, along the coast of Holland and Germany. When local wars there prevented a successful mission, they returned to England, but Winfred's concern continued. A few years later he returned to Friesland, making a number of converts to the Christian faith.

Instead of feeling satisfied, Winfrid's concern for the people grew even larger. So, after only three years, he went to Rome to ask permission to bring the Gospel to *all* of Germany. Pope Gregory II, impressed with Winfrid's missionary vision, gave Winfrid a new name (Boniface, which means "he who does good") and sent him back as apostle to all the German peoples. Boniface took on the assignment with enthusiasm and traveled into German lands where pagan ways still prevailed.

The incident behind Boniface's symbols of tree and ax took place near the town of Geismar on a tall hill, Mount Gudenberg. There stood an oak tree supposedly sacred to the Teutonic god Thor. Boniface's announcement that he would cut it down astonished the local pagan people. They were sure that he would immediately be struck dead. With many watching, Boniface put his ax to the tree, and after a few of his solid strokes, it fell, splitting into four pieces. Boniface and his coworkers gathered up the wood and built a chapel on the site. Many in that region became Christians after the ax incident.

As years passed, Boniface traveled through all the German lands, establishing schools, monasteries, and churches. Yet as busy as he was, he never forgot about Friesland. When he was almost 80 years old and could have retired comfortably, Boniface headed back to Friesland because the people there had reverted to pagan ways. He set up a Christian learning center near the village of Dokkum, where he taught the faith with patience and success—until some local people suspected that Boniface was hoarding treasures. One day early in June they came to his tent, murdered the elderly man, and looked for the treasure. They found only some books, never discovering that the treasure was the Gospel message written down on the pages, that through Jesus alone we are saved from our sins.

Boniface was buried at Fulda, at a monastery he had established, where his tomb and the book he was holding when he died remain to this day. Boniface's love for the German people cost him his life, just as the Savior laid down his life for all of us. Boniface, the apostle with the ax, is remembered on June 5.

Almighty God, give us a missionary spirit that will not rest until all people hear of your love. Make us oaks of righteousness in our day, and finally call us to our place with the saints in light. We ask this for Jesus' sake. Amen.

You may also want to pray for the church in Germany.

Saint Bridget
(1303–1373)

"Surely, I Am with You Always"

But be sure to fear the LORD and serve him faithfully with all your heart; consider what great things he has done for you. 1 Samuel 12:24

Bridget was familiar with death and tragedy. Her mother died when she was young. She became a widow early in her life. Two of her eight children died at young ages; others had bad marriages or became involved in affairs. Many people in her home country died from a plague during her lifetime. Clearly, her life was not a fairy tale, yet by her faith she made the best of changing situations. She became one of the most notable Scandinavian women of the 14th century, one well remembered throughout her native Sweden for her ability to deal with tragedy and heartache without losing trust in God.

Bridget, or Birgitta as she is called in Swedish, was born into a noble family, the daughter of a "lawman," a local ruler in medieval Sweden. After her mother died, she was raised by an aunt until she married at the age of 14. Although she did not want to become a bride at that age, she found happiness in her marriage to Ulf Godmarsson. Known for her education and piety, she was appointed chief lady-in-waiting to the newly married Swedish queen, Blanche.

Even at a young age, Bridget was a woman of influence. At her insistence, King Magnus brought humane changes to Sweden, including the decree that no child born of a Christian father or mother could be "held as a thrall" (kept as a slave). Bridget tended the sick and established a religious center at Vadstena, a castle she had been given by the royal family. After becoming a widow, she gave her inherited fortune to her family and to the poor, keeping enough money only to "live simply and dress modestly."

After receiving divine visions, Bridget decided that her work in Sweden was done. Moving to the center of church activity at Rome, she established an order of Christian women whose lives were given to prayer and charity in the name of Christ. Though she never saw her native country again, she was strengthened by this confidence: "God, who drew thee out of the nest, will care for thee till death."

At times, we too may find ourselves in a situation that takes us away from familiar surroundings. Like Bridget, we may find ourselves experiencing family problems, illness, or disappointments. Even then and there God is with us, promising the sustaining love we find shown in the suffering and death of Jesus Christ for us.

Until the time of her death, Bridget continued faithfully to serve the Lord, making religious pilgrimages and counseling leaders of the church. After a year of severe illness, she died at Rome in the year 1373 on July 23, which is now her date on the church calendar.

Give us a lasting vision of your love and care for us, Lord. Help us, as the saints of these times, to bring glory to you. We ask this in the name of Jesus, our abiding Savior. Amen.

You might also want to pray for those experiencing heartache and those who find themselves away from familiar surroundings.

Saint Cecelia
(c. 214–c. 230)

Singing with the Saints

Let the word of Christ dwell in you richly as you teach and admonish one another with all wisdom, and as you sing psalms, hymns and spiritual songs with gratitude in your hearts to God. Colossians 3:16

The dates next to her name remind us that Cecelia is numbered among the teenage saints. She was the young Roman martyr who gave up her life rather than renounce her faith in Jesus as Savior and Lord. Cecelia is remembered for her music—for the hymns and psalms she sang to express and to support her faith. She knew the special strength found in words of belief combined with music, a power available to all of us through the hymns of the church.

History and tradition combine to tell us the story of Saint Cecelia. Born near the beginning of the third century, she grew up in the patrician class, accustomed to wealth and social standing. She also grew up as a follower of Jesus. When she came to marriageable age in her early teens, Cecelia told her family that she did not wish to marry but rather wanted to remain a virgin and dedicate her life to Christian service. Her family would not hear of that. They announced her engagement to a young pagan named Valerian and arranged for the wedding feast.

Cecelia was not a happy bride. While the guests merrily danced and carried on to wedding tunes, Cecelia sat in a corner of the room, singing psalms and songs to God. Making the best of a married state she did not choose, Cecelia set out to convert her husband to Christianity. In a very short while, both he and his brother, Tibertius, were baptized and became active in the expanding but still secret church at Rome.

Happy earthly endings are hard to come by in the first Christian centuries. Valerian and Tibertius risked their lives to claim the bodies of Christians who had been martyred so that they could be properly buried, even though that was illegal. Hostile authorities quickly arrested the two young men. After they were tried, convicted, and executed, Cecelia took up their work, finding fit burial places for her family and other martyrs. Even in her times of grief, she continued singing her psalms, hymns, and spiritual songs.Before long, Cecelia also was arrested, tried, convicted, and executed for her faith. Before she died she willed all of her goods to the poor and requested that her home become a place for worship.

It is not always easy to sing to God when life challenges or disappoints us, but God has promised us his lasting love, the very love he showed fully in the death of his Son Jesus for our sins. He will support us throughout our lives, through our death, and then into eternity. Tradition tells us that although Cecelia suffered a prolonged and painful execution, she died with words of blessing and hymns of praise on her young lips. She knew she had songs yet to sing at the heavenly throne of Jesus, the Lamb of God. We remember her as we think of the saints in glory on her feast day, November 22.

Give us songs for you in our day, Lord. Fill our lives with words and music, with hymns and praise. Even when discouragements and sorrows come our way, supply us with melodies and words to strengthen our spirits and encourage our hearts. In Jesus' name we make our prayer. Amen.

You might also want to pray for church musicians and teenagers.

Saint Clement
(c. 35–c. 100)

Truly a Disciple's Disciple

Consequently, you are no longer foreigners and aliens, but fellow citizens with God's people and members of God's household, built on the foundation of the apostles and prophets, with Christ Jesus himself as the chief cornerstone. Ephesians 2:19–20

Starting up an organization is hardly ever easy. There are rules to be established, officers to be chosen, and perhaps a constitution to be written. And usually not everyone agrees with everything being done. Even the work and the workings of the church need a special measure of patience and prayer, something that has been true since the very first century.

Clement of Rome used both patience and prayer as he gave shape to the fledgling Christian church. Sharing firsthand information received from the apostles, he established the pattern of authority that governed the Christian movement in the first and second centuries. This initiative established the importance of keeping

Christ at the center of working together as members of his body, the church.

Clement's early life is lost to history. Some traditions suggest that he was baptized by Saint Peter; others identify him with the Clement mentioned by Saint Paul in Philippians 4:3. It is certain that Clement was active in the Roman church and that, according to Saint Irenaeus, he "had seen and consorted with the blessed apostles." Clement's conversations with the disciples and his knowledge of the Christian writings being circulated made him a singular source of information and authority.

As the first century ended, the Christian church had grown both in numbers and in activity. Because the last of the apostles, the eyewitnesses of Jesus, were dying off, people they had appointed were filling leadership roles in the local congregations. Not everyone wanted to accept the new leadership, especially not the Corinthians. To address the situation there, Clement wrote a long letter to Corinth, emphasizing the importance of obedience to ordained authority. He based it on the Gospel message, writing, "Let us note what is good, what is pleasing and acceptable to him who made us. Let us fix our eyes on the blood of Christ and let us realize how precious it is to his Father, since it was poured out for our salvation and brought the grace of repentance to the whole world" (1 Clement 6:31). Apparently Clement's epistle met with acceptance at Corinth. People read it in the church there and at churches in the area around the Mediterranean Sea.

Through his letter, Clement had added an important building block to the structure we know as the church.

Keeping focused on the sacrificial love of God in Christ Jesus is just as important now as it was in the first century. God's love has not lessened or been diluted as the centuries have passed; His care for us in our challenging times is just as solid as it was for his faithful people in Clement's day.

As with many other first Christians, Clement endured a martyr's death when, having been exiled by Roman authorities to work in the mines near the Crimean Sea, he was dropped into deep water with an anchor around his neck. Clement displayed Christlike love for the church, serving as an inspiration for us to care for the only organization built on the foundation of the prophets and apostles, with Christ Jesus as the cornerstone. November 23 is Clement's day on the church calendar.

Holy Spirit, Designer of the church, make us builders in our generation. Help us honor the memory of previous builders, remembering their sacrifice and following their example of devotion and dedication. In Jesus' name we pray. Amen.

You may also want to pray that the Lord will enable you to remain focused on his sacrificial love in Christ.

Saint Columba
(c. 521–597)

On Wings of Praise

We know that in all things God works for the good of those who love him, who have been called according to his purpose. Romans 8:28

One of the most striking figures in the era of the expanding church was named for a bird: Columba, whose name means "dove." What a difference his life made! He took a bad situation, turned it into a challenge, and used it to God's glory. Saint Columba's biographer, Adamnan, tells us that Columba was tall, dark haired, and fair skinned, with a voice "so loud and melodious it could be heard a mile off." He had "eyes the color of gray sea water," and he was "loving to everyone, happy-faced, rejoicing in his inmost heart with the joy of the Holy Spirit." And that is as it should be—for *saint* means "blessed," and *blessed* means "happy." Columba, or Columkille as he is known in his native Ireland, found happiness in focusing the energy of his life on doing Christ-honoring deeds.

Born into a royal Irish family, Columba followed his early inclination to become a priest. His placid, productive, and unremarkable life changed when he became involved in an Irish clan feud. Carrying out one of his priestly duties, he extended the hospitality of his monastery to a relative, Prince Curnan, who had fatally injured a rival during a hurling match, a traditional Celtic sport. Seeking total revenge, the slain rival's tribe ignored the sanctuary Columba offered Curnan and killed the prince at the monastery, a place supposedly exempt from bloodshed. The ensuing family war left 3,000 dead. By some logic of those times, a meeting of church leaders held Columba responsible for all of the deaths. Then 42 years old, he decided to leave Ireland and, in remorse, vowed to convert 3,000 pagans.

The mission target for Columba was Scotland, the land of his ancestors, where many Picts and Scots still lived according to pagan ways. Assisted by 12 relatives, Columba established a monastery on the island of Iona, just off the Scottish coast, as the base for his Gospel-spreading operations. From there, Columba and his monks shared the wonderful message of God's forgiving love in Jesus Christ through Britain and beyond, into the far corners of Europe.

From his earliest years, Columba found special joy in copying Bible manuscripts. Under his supervision, monks at Iona and Kells, another of Columba's many monasteries, developed the copying of Bibles by hand into a wonderful art form called "illuminated manuscripts." You might enjoy looking into an art history book that devotes a section to the copyists of the early

Middle Ages, whose work combined biblical truth with artistic beauty.

On June 8, 597, Columba was copying verses 9 and 10 of Psalm 34. After he had written "those who seek the LORD lack no good thing," he stopped his pen and turned the work over to his cousin, Baithin. In a way, these words of the psalmist summarized Columba's life. Columba, the dove of the church, died the next day. An example of faithful goal-setting and lifelong Christian witness, Columba and his ministry are celebrated on the church calendar each June 9.

Help us to see the design of goodness you have imprinted on our lives, gracious Lord. Bless our days with a joy that illuminates all we do and say. No matter what situations come along, may we continue to bring you glory. In Jesus' name we pray. Amen.

You may also want to pray for the church in Scotland and for historians.

Saint Elizabeth
(c. 1207–1231)

Charity Begins at Home

As God's chosen people, holy and dearly loved, clothe yourselves with compassion, kindness, humility, gentleness and patience. ... And over all these virtues put on love, which binds them all together in perfect unity. Colossians 3:12, 14

Saint Elizabeth is a shooting star in the sky of the saints, a medieval woman of great character and unwavering faith. Her 24 years on earth knew both joy and tragedy. Her life glowed brightly as she became a devoted wife and mother of four children, a benevolent and popular queen, and a one-person charity crusade in Thuringia, a mountainous area in the heartland of Germany. Yet by the age of 20, Elizabeth was a widow; four years later she was dead.

Two peoples claim Elizabeth as a special saint: the Germans and Hungarians. Hungary claims her because she was born a princess and spent the first four years of her life there. At that tender age, her father, King Andrew, took her far from home to the Wartburg Castle near the city of Eisenach, a fortress made famous a few centuries later as a place of refuge for Martin Luther during the Reformation era. The king had made a contract for her to marry Ludwig, a son of the local Landgrave. Such politically arranged marriages were common in the 13th century. Frequently the betrothed children were educated by the same tutors and spent hours together learning the etiquette of the court. Actual romance in these situations was rare. However, Ludwig and Elizabeth developed strong bonds of affection and were married when she was 14. Ludwig already had succeeded his father as ruler of Thuringia, so Elizabeth shared that rule as his wife. Germany claims Elizabeth because of her life as an outstanding Christian queen.

Her six-year reign is still remembered in Thuringia. Not only did she have four children in those years, but she made it her priority to fill the castle and countryside with her charity. She built hospitals for the poor, fed the hungry from the Wartburg's kitchen, dressed orphans warmly in wintertime, and even gave up her own royal bed to a leper when one of the hospices she had established became overcrowded. Elizabeth took to heart the words of Jesus, "Whatever you did for one of the least of these brothers of mine, you did for me" (Matthew 25:40). She loved the unlovable, just as Jesus loved us in our sinfulness and gave his life for us. Demonstrating the charity Saint Paul commended to the Colossians, she bound her virtues together with love.

Not everyone in the royal family supported Elizabeth's generous sharing from the royal treasury. When Ludwig died of the plague while traveling with the Fifth

Crusade to the Holy Land, Elizabeth's brother-in-law evicted her and the four children from the Wartburg. She was 20 years old. Even in this sad situation, Elizabeth maintained her nobility and her faith. After making living arrangements for each of her children, she entered a religious order. The rest of her life was spent caring for the sick at Marburg, Germany, making clothes for the needy, and fishing in local streams when food for her patients ran low. Only four years after her death (brought on by her austere lifestyle), she was officially named a saint of the church and added to the church calendar on November 17, the day of her death in 1231.

Gracious God and giver of all good gifts, help us find fulfillment in charity. Let your Holy Spirit guide us as we invest our time and share our possessions so that the resources of our lives are well spent. In Jesus' name we pray. Amen.

You might also want to pray for medical caregivers and for social workers.

Saint Francis of Assisi

(c. 1181–1226)

Herald of the Great King

Has not God chosen those who are poor in the eyes of the world to be rich in faith and to inherit the kingdom he promised those who love him? James 2:5

Saint Francis seems to be everywhere! We see his likeness on greeting cards, in portrait displays, and even as statues in gardens and greenhouses. Usually he is pictured in a monk's robe with a collection of animals around him and perhaps a bird on his shoulder. Although his image may be familiar, his personal history may not be.

Born in the year 1181 or 1182 into a wealthy Italian family at Assisi, Francis had the best of everything. In his younger years he enjoyed a life filled with music, friends, parties, and learning the merchant trade from his father. Despite the carefree pleasantness of his childhood and young adulthood, Francis felt unsettled and unsure of what to do with the rest of his life.

When he was 21, after a year away from home as a prisoner captured in a local war, Francis returned to

Assisi a changed person. The dashing young merchant's son had become deeply religious, no longer caring about the riches due him as his father's heir. Instead, he cared about churches that needed repair, poor people who needed assistance, and lepers who needed someone to care for them. Francis had found his calling as a disciple of Jesus for his time and place.

In Matthew's gospel, chapter 10, Jesus sends out his disciples with no gold or silver or extra cloak or even sandals. Inspired by this and other Bible sections, Francis outlined a life of complete self-denial. The people of his time and place took to heart Francis' invitation to faithful poverty. By the year 1215 his followers numbered in the thousands. Many Franciscans (as they were later called) went on missionary journeys, preaching repentance and the love of God revealed in Christ Jesus and his sacrifice on the cross. Others, both women and men, formed religious houses throughout Europe where hospitality was offered and charity was extended. Meanwhile, Francis kept on preaching and praying and singing, calling himself "the herald of the great King." His ability to get along with animals became legendary; he was known for addressing all creatures and even the forces of nature as brother and sister. One time at Alviano, when loudly chirping birds interrupted his preaching, he said simply, "Little sister swallows, it is now my turn to speak; you have been talking enough all this time." And the birds became silent.

In his final years, Francis established the custom of the Christmas crèche, sent members of his religious order as mediators and peacemakers to settle civil disputes and other problems, and composed the "Canti-cle of the Sun," the first religious poem in the Italian language. Often set to music, this canticle expresses his love for God's creation and his joy at the wonders of life. Sharing that wonder, we thank God for Saint Francis, remembering him especially on October 4, when he appears on the church calendar.

God our Creator, help us to find richness in all of your creation and to discover joy in serving the needs of others. Give us vision to be brotherly and sisterly to your creation, but especially to all other people, who share this earth with us. We ask this for the sake of Jesus, our Brother and Savior. Amen.

You may also want to pray for humility and for good stewardship of God's creation.

Gabriel

God's Special Messenger

The angel answered: "I am Gabriel. I stand in the presence of God, and I have been sent to speak to you and to tell you this good news." Luke 1:19

In "Before the Paling of the Stars," the poem which inspired this book, Christina Rossetti invites us to worship the Christ Child: "Let us kneel with Mary maid, with Joseph bent and hoary, with saint and angel, ox and ass, to hail the King of glory." Among the angels we can envision at the mangerside is Gabriel, God's special messenger. The Bible mentions countless angels, yet names very few of them. Gabriel, meaning "strong one of God," appears in both the Old and New Testaments. In human form, he shared a vision of the future with Daniel, announcing the good news that history would end in God's final victory (Daniel 8:16). Later, Gabriel came to the prophet "in person" to reassure him that God's Anointed One would come (Daniel 9:21). For Daniel this was wonderful news.

Gabriel always brings good news. In the gospel of Saint Luke, chapter 1, he tells of two special births: of Jesus (Luke 1:31) and of Jesus' cousin and forerunner

John (Luke 1:13). The traditional symbol for Gabriel, the lily, represents purity and the promise of new life through the power of God. Often artists place a lily in Gabriel's hand as they portray the annunciation to Mary.

The new life proclaimed to Mary by Gabriel came in the person of Jesus Christ, who by his death and resurrection grants us forgiveness of sins and the assurance of the life eternal in the presence of God already enjoyed by the angels. In one of his sermons, Martin Luther comments on our relationship with the angels, saying, "Christ is our Brother, and we are his heirs. And the dear angels, such as Michael and Gabriel, are not to be our masters but our brothers and servants, for they also call God their Father, just as we do. This is a grand and overpowering thought!"

That God has given angels such as Gabriel charge of us, to help and protect us, is amazing. In the psalms we read: "If you make the Most High your dwelling—even the LORD, who is my refuge—then no harm will befall you. ... For he will command his angels concerning you to guard you in all your ways; they will lift you up in their hands" (Psalm 91:9, 11–12). Jesus used this promise as he dealt with temptation, and we read that when he had overcome his temptations, "angels came and attended him" (Matthew 4:11). God's angels are all around, to protect and defend us and to join with us in praise. God's angels not only bring, but are good news!

Lord of earth and heaven, we bless you for the caring ministry of Gabriel and all the angels that touch our lives. Make us aware of your messages, and give us a sense of wonder and joy in the ways you communicate with us. In Jesus' name we pray. Amen.

You may also want to pray for missionaries, that the Lord would send guardian angels to protect them from harm and danger.

Saint Gregory
(c. 540–604)

Servant of the Servants

We are God's workmanship, created in Christ Jesus to do good works, which God prepared in advance for us to do. Ephesians 2:10

Although most of us have only one or a few special gifts or abilities, a few people seem to be able to do almost everything well. Gregory was one of those people. He dominated both the history of the Christian church and secular events in western Europe at the close of the sixth century. Gregory was an administrator, a missionary, and a musician as well as a pastor. Rome reached the lowest point in its history around the time Gregory was born in that city. Constantly faced with enemy invasions, plagues, and pillage, only 500 residents remained in what had been the glorious city, where 150,000 people could watch events at one time in the Circus Maximus. Gregory decided to do something about the situation. Working his way up through the ranks of what was left of the local government, he became mayor of Rome in 573. Working tirelessly, he managed to improve conditions, and he even restored some of Rome's faded glory.

After his term as mayor, Gregory gave the church his extensive landholdings in Sicily and converted his Roman villa into a monastery. He would have been content to remain living there, but God had other uses for his gifts and talents. Just as he had moved up through the levels of civil servants, so Gregory rose in the ranks of church workers, becoming bishop of Rome on September 3, 590.

Gregory was concerned that people throughout Europe should hear the Gospel message. One day when he saw some captives from England in the Roman slave market, he inquired from where these fair-skinned, light-haired people had come. "They are Angles," he was told. "They ought to become angels," he replied. And he made plans to start a special mission journey to England. Like Jesus, who made the ultimate sacrifice of love by coming to earth in person and winning forgiveness of sins by his death, Gregory was willing to sacrifice his resources, career, and perhaps even his life to go personally to England with the Good News of salvation. Circumstances at Rome, however, prevented that. Instead, in 596, Saint Austin of Canterbury and a group of Angle slaves, purchased by Gregory and trained as monks for their homeland, firmly established Christianity in Britain.

Interested in all areas of achievement, Gregory encouraged the use of chant and antiphons in the church and began the Schola Cantorum (school for church singers) at Rome. As a pastor, he wrote a number of books about church practices and established the church-year calendar most Christians in the Western world still follow today.

Through all of his years of leadership, Gregory maintained a perspective on his purpose in life, calling himself "servant of the servants of God." His example of creative service is one for all Christians to follow in their own times and ways. Although he died on March 12 in 604, his calendar date is most frequently observed on September 3, which commemorates his being named bishop at Rome.

Gracious Lord, you are the giver of all talents and abilities. Whatever our gifts may be, inspire us to use them to your glory. Help us find satisfaction and joy in being servants of the servants of God around us. In Jesus' name we pray. Amen.

You might also want to pray for pastors and the worship life of the church.

Saint Helena
(c. 255–c. 329)

Lifting High the Cross

Even to your old age and gray hairs I am he, I am he who will sustain you. Isaiah 46:4

Older saints can get things done. That truth is demonstrated by Saint Helena, one of the most amazing Christian women of the fourth century (or of any century, for that matter). Empress, wife, mother, world traveler, benefactress, builder, patroness of Christian learning, amateur archaeologist, discoverer of holy places—Helena was all these and more.

At age 18 Helena met a Roman general named Constantius Chlorus. A brief courtship resulted in marriage for this lowly born girl from far-off Bithynia. Constantius advanced in his career and eventually was named emperor. Obliged to marry into the Roman political establishment because of his high office, he divorced Helena and left her to raise their son, Constantine, on her own. After his father's death, Constantine became emperor at the age of 32. Honoring his long-suffering mother, he named her as his empress. Just over 50 years old, she suddenly became the most important and influential woman in the world of her time.

Called to believe by the Holy Spirit, Helena was baptized into Christ and his church at the age of 63. Her growing faith changed her values and goals, and she, in turn, changed the religious shape of the Roman world. Helena supported the faith. She promoted the faith. And she lived the faith. Never regarding herself as above God's commandments or his people, she attended worship regularly, standing elbow to elbow with common Christians, dressed in the simple clothes of the poor. The famed church historian Eusebius wrote of Helena, "Though empress of the world and mistress of the empire, she looked upon herself as servant of the handmaids of Christ."

As Helena got older, she got better. When she was in her 70s, Constantine sent her to the Holy Land to identify and oversee sites sacred to Christians. When she toured Jerusalem and Bethlehem, Helena didn't like what she discovered. The places most sacred to Christians had been altered or were in ruins. Jesus' birthplace had been rededicated to the Roman god Adonis; a temple to Venus stood on Calvary, where Jesus had died for the sins of the world. Using the treasury of the empire, Helena authorized the building of Christian basilica-style churches, restoring many sacred locations. Some parts of the building projects she personally supervised can still be seen today.

Helena rediscovered many sites and objects of great value that had been lost to Christians of all times. Some traditions suggest that she found the wooden post that had been part of the cross of Jesus. Yet a few years after her death, Saint Ambrose wrote that "she worshipped not the wood, but the king who hung on that wood," who, as Saint Paul says, "humbled himself and became obedient to death—even death on a cross" (Philippians 2:8). Whether or not we ever physically get to see the place where Jesus died and rose again, as Helena did, we know that what happened there was for us and for our salvation.

Saint Helena lived her "golden years" in a golden way, and as a result, her contributions and discoveries continue to bless the church. Her special day on the calendar is August 18.

Lord of all generations, make us faith-filled discoverers whatever our age. Grant us trust in you and excitement about your work, so that we lift high your cross in our world today. In Jesus' wonderful name we pray. Amen.

You may also want to pray for the aged and for the church in the Holy Land.

Saint Hilary
(c. 310–368)

With a Song in His Heart

My heart is steadfast, O God, my heart is steadfast; I will sing and make music. … I will praise you, O Lord, among the nations; I will sing of you among the peoples.
Psalm 57:7, 9

What do you do when you've got time on your hands? Do you look at your watch or look at the needs of those around you? Hilary, a Christian bishop in exile, took the second option, solving a problem for Christians in Asia Minor in the middle of the fourth century. The problem was simple: Arians, opponents of orthodox believers, were using newly composed hymns to appeal to people and make converts. (See "Saint Athanasius.") Hilary countered by putting biblical words and familiar music together for the orthodox believers. He was so successful that he came to be known as "The Hammer of the Arians."

Having become a Christian believer later in life, Hilary had risen quickly to the office of bishop in

Poitiers, Gaul (now France), despite his own personal objections. Through years of Scripture study, reflection, and prayer, the Lord had led him to be baptized, along with his wife and their daughter, Apra. A convinced convert and a ready promoter of the faith he held, Hilary became involved in the doctrinal controversies of the church at the beginning of the fourth century. Eventually his zeal got him in trouble with Emperor Constantius, and he was banished from Gaul and transported to Asia Minor, far from his home and family.

Finding something to do in exile might challenge some people. Hilary decided to use his time creatively by giving the opponents of orthodox Christianity some musical competition. Taking the sturdy rhythms and solid melodies of Roman marching songs, he set to music the basics of the true faith. Hilary picked up where the psalm writers had left off, filling his songs with the Good News that Jesus Christ, God in the flesh, loved us and gave himself as a sacrifice for our sins. The message filled the music, and the music made the message even more memorable.

Hilary's hymns were instant hits. People got together in the evenings and sang them again and again. An early tradition in worship had been expanded and enhanced, all because of an exiled bishop with time on his hands and a song in his heart. Of the many hymns authored by Hilary, only three remain today: one telling of Jesus' temptations by Satan, another for the Easter season, and the third about the Trinity, a song that continues on for 70 stanzas.

Eventually Hilary was able to return to his home in Gaul. Sharing his faith whenever he could, he continued writing and composing until the end of his days. The church calendar day generally observed for Hilary of Poitiers is January 13.

Keep our hearts steadfast and our voices tuneful, Lord. Blend our hymns with the music of psalmists and writers of the past, with the choirs of saints today, and with the harmonies of the angels in praise yet to be. In Jesus' name we pray. Amen.

You might also want to pray that pure doctrine will be preserved in the church and that hymns new and old may inspire each generation.

Saint Hilda
(614–680)

A Gift for Discovering Gifts

Those who are wise will shine like the brightness of the heavens, and those who lead many to righteousness, like the stars for ever and ever. Daniel 12:3

Sometimes the least known saints turn out to be the most memorable. Hilda is that kind of a saint. Born in Great Britain shortly after the year 600, she lived her life during an almost-forgotten era. Yet her devotion to the Christian faith and to education in her time continues to influence all English-speaking countries, including ours. The light of Hilda's contributions still shines brightly.

During the seventh century (part of the Dark Ages), feuds, battles, and wars made life unsettled and generally unpleasant throughout Europe. This was especially true around Whitby, England, where Hilda served as an abbess, the leader of a religious house for both women and men. In those harsh years, few people except the wealthy had time for formal learning. Or so most everyone believed. However, Hilda didn't agree. She encouraged everybody she met to continue learning throughout their lives, whatever their station or situation. Continuing our own education, especially our growth in the knowledge and love of our Lord Jesus, is a good goal for every age of our lives.

One of the people Hilda influenced was Caedmon, a herdsman and keeper of the abbey grounds at Whitby. One night he dreamed that he was called to be a "singer of creation," and so he began to sing praise to God, even though he had no musical background or training. Hilda heard about Caedmon and his special songs. She brought him into the monastery, where he could write poetry and compose his tunes full time. It was a wise move on her part. Caedmon the farmhand became Caedmon the minstrel and the father of poetry in the English language. Hilda's small encouragement made a big difference.

How are we at encouraging people to use their gifts to the glory of God? Many people have first heard the Gospel message of God's love in Jesus Christ because some "Hilda" invited them to church to sing or to play an instrument or to participate in a reading or drama. Whom can you invite? Someone you know could be greatly blessed by your encouragement.

By finding the best in the people around her and developing their gifts, Hilda reflected Christ himself, who went into the darkness of death to bring us eternal light and the promise of fulfilling life. The words of the prophet Daniel in today's passage describe Hilda of

Whitby, a wise woman who by her encouragement led many to righteousness and the full use of their talents to the glory of God. She is remembered by the church on November 17.

Ever-helpful Lord, we bless you for our teachers and examples, those women and men who encourage us throughout our years. Show us ways to encourage others by our words and our actions, to your praise and your glory forever. Amen.

You might also want to pray for educational institutions and endeavors.

Saint Hippolytus
(c. 170–c. 236)

A Picture of Worship

I meditate on your precepts and consider your ways. I delight in your decrees; I will not neglect your word. Psalm 119:15–16

"Write what you see," some English teachers tell their students. Not only does that improve one's writing, it also can become a special blessing to people who live long after you. Thanks to Hippolytus, writer of *The Apostolic Tradition* around the year 215, we have a clear and insightful look at the early church and its worship life. *The Apostolic Tradition* tells about church discipline, customs, and ceremonies and serves as a "still photo" of what it was like to attend Christian worship at Rome in those days.

Not that much is known about Hippolytus as a person. Probably born in Asia Minor, he became a priest in the Roman Church. Caught up in church politics, he was exiled to the island of Sardinia, where, tradition tells us, he died a martyr's death. Perhaps that is all we would know about Hippolytus, had not some Roman workmen in 1551 uncovered the long-buried statue of this churchman seated on a chair. Inscribed on the sides of the chair was a listing of his writings. Dating from the saint's lifetime, this "saint statue" is the oldest of its kind ever found. Included in the works of Hippolytus are commentaries on Daniel, Song of Songs, and Psalms. These writings, the first Christian commentaries on Old Testament books, help us see how Christians then linked the Old and New Testaments. Both sections of the Bible point us to Jesus as the one who fulfills God's plan and saves us from our sins. That Good News of salvation is retold and reflected in our worship each week.

The picture of worship in the third century contains much that we would recognize from an order of service today. Some parts, however, such as the sharing of a cup of water and a cup of milk mixed with honey at the celebration of the Lord's Supper, would not be familiar. Hippolytus reflects in detail the very earliest times in church history. Traditional in his outlook, he opposed those who wanted to augment the worship life of the church with "new fasts and feasts, abstinences, and diets of radishes."

In all of his writings, Hippolytus delights in the Word of the Lord and advocates high standards for worship. That he took the time to write down his observations in such a helpful way has been a blessing, one that might well inspire you to write about your faith and life for sharing with generations yet to come. Hippolytus' day on the church calendar is August 13.

One prayer Hippolytus records includes these words:

O God, grant that we may praise and glorify you through your Son Jesus Christ, through whom be glory and honor to you with the Holy Spirit in your holy church now and forever and world without end. Amen.

You may also want to pray for those who communicate the Gospel through all types of media.

Saint Ignatius
(c. 40–107)

Preserve the Faith

Since an overseer [a bishop] is entrusted with God's work, he must be blameless. ... He must hold firmly to the trustworthy message as it has been taught, so that he can encourage others by sound doctrine and refute those who oppose it. Titus 1:7, 9

Today we easily take for granted the creeds of the church, thinking that Christians of all time have confessed these statements of faith as we do. They have not. Creeds were developed during the first Christian centuries as responses to doctrinal controversies in the early church. In the initial generations after Jesus' ascension, people depended on their local bishops to outline the basics of the faith for them. They trusted the bishop for guidance, instruction, and spiritual care. Through these early years, the office of bishop grew in its scope and in its authority as the Christian community expanded. Choosing a bishop was an important decision!

Ignatius of Antioch was an ideal bishop. Tradition tells us that the apostles Peter and Paul chose him for leadership in the church of Syria. The historical record confirms that he served as bishop there for 40 years. During many of those years both Jews and Gentiles persecuted the believers in Syria. Through encouraging sermons, Ignatius focused his people on maintaining the unity of faith, urging them to gather frequently for the Lord's Supper. He called Holy Communion "the flesh of Christ," "the gift of God," and "the medicine of immortality."

Ignatius had the surname Theophorus, which means God-bearer. He lived out the meaning of his name as he carried the message of God's love in Jesus Christ every day of his ministry until wild beasts, at the command of Emperor Trajan, killed the aged bishop during the public games at the colosseum in Rome. He knew and trusted this love of God in Christ Jesus. On his journey from Antioch to Rome as a prisoner, Ignatius wrote seven letters, which not only leave behind his testimony of belief but also share a full picture of the church in its infancy. The letters give us a valuable "bishop's eye view" of our ancestors in the faith from 20 centuries ago.

In these final letters, Ignatius wrote that Christians should respect and listen to their ordained leaders. He counseled the Ephesians, "Hence it is fitting for you to set yourselves in harmony with the mind of the bishop, as indeed you do. For your noble presbytery, worthy of God, is attuned to the bishop, even as the strings to a lyre. And thus by means of your accord and harmonious love, Jesus Christ is sung." What a strong witness when people and leaders work positively together under the lordship of Jesus Christ, who is "the Shepherd and Overseer [Bishop] of your souls" (1 Peter 2:25)!

Ignatius can encourage us in our faith through his grand vision of the church, being the first Christian writer to call it "catholic," meaning worldwide or universal. Bishop Ignatius serves as a model for Christian leadership and responsible church membership for the ages. His day on the church calendar is observed around the world on the day of his death, December 20, the last day of the public games at Rome in A.D. 107.

Lord of the church, bless us in our day with fearless leaders and faithful people, that the church may continue to witness to you in both word and deed. Make us God-bearers who joyfully confess your name and live to your glory. Through Jesus, the way, the truth, and the life, we pray. Amen.

You may also want to pray for the church in all of the world.

Saint Jerome
(c. 345–420)

Words and More Wonderful Words

How sweet are your words to my taste, sweeter than honey to my mouth! … Your word is a lamp to my feet and a light for my path. Psalm 119:103, 105

Skill in using a certain kind of raw material is the hallmark of a craftsman. Blacksmiths work with iron; silversmiths work with precious metals; wordsmiths work with words. Saint Jerome was an outstanding wordsmith. Not only did he know countless words in many languages, but more importantly he used his gift of language in the Lord's work. Every time we pick up a Bible and read from it, we are in debt to Jerome: translator, wordsmith, and singular saint.

Jerome's gift for words was developed at an early age. Born in an Adriatic seacoast town, he headed off to Rome for his formal education. In those days, ability to use words well was the key to prestige and success. Jerome studied hard and learned quickly yet somehow never found a direction for his life in the classroom. Restless and searching, he set out to travel.

Jerome's journeys took him from far up in France to far down in Egypt. In each new location he added to his collection of languages and words. From a Jewish-Christian monk he learned Hebrew, the language of the Old Testament, which made him one of the few Christians at that time who could read the words of the prophets in the original languages. The more he read from the Scriptures, the stronger his faith grew. Jerome at last discovered his life's work: to be a wordsmith for the Lord.

Damasus, the leader of the Roman Church, recognized Jerome's special ability with words. He invited the young scholar to translate the New Testament from Greek into Latin, the one language spoken throughout the Western world at that time. Jerome's complete translation of the Bible from Greek and Hebrew was called the Vulgate, because it put Scripture into the common (vulgar, as it was known) language of the day. Working patiently and precisely, Jerome rejoiced in the Word of the Lord in the same way as did the psalmist centuries before. God's people can always rejoice in being close to him through his Word, which tells of his wonderful plan of redemption for all the people of the world through the cross of Jesus Christ.

Jerome's work set a pattern for later common-language translations, including Luther's Bible texts and the many English versions now available. Vocabulary choices and sentence structures shaped by Jerome the wordsmith are still echoed today in Scripture readings throughout the world. After a full and productive life, Jerome died in Bethlehem in the year 420. His day on the church calendar is September 30.

Lord, we thank you for writers, copyists, and translators who have brought the Bible to us. May your Word always be a lamp to our feet, enlightening our pathways through all of life. In Jesus' name we pray. Amen.

You might also want to pray for Bible translators, scholars, and students.

Saint John Chrysostom
(c. 347–407)

Better than a Silver Tongue

A word aptly spoken is like apples of gold in settings of silver. Proverbs 25:11

Are you a speaker of golden words? Do you easily find the right thing to say for every occasion? Few people do. In the fourth century, one of those rare people with a special gift of communication was John, the bishop of Constantinople. John preached such powerful and moving sermons that after his death he was given the nickname "Chrysostom," which means "golden-mouthed." Maybe we will never get that kind of nickname. Still, we can choose and use our words to the glory of God, following the example of John.

A major leader in the era of the expanding church, John grew up in Antioch, one of the urban centers of the Roman Empire. At that time Antioch, located in what now is Turkey, was half pagan and half Christian. John's family reflected the community. His father was a non-Christian military leader and his mother a pious Christian named Anthusa. After being educated for a career as a lawyer, John changed his vocation and pursued the religious life instead. Two years in the mountains as a hermit on a religious retreat led him to conclude that he would fit better in an urban setting back in his hometown, where there were people to speak with and to preach to. Once back home, he moved through a number of church offices, including acolyte and lector. Finally, he was named presbyter and, as such, was given the privilege of preaching on a regular basis.

Week after week, John's golden words sounded throughout the church. People from all over the region flocked to Antioch to hear the little man who spoke so fervently and taught the Scriptures so clearly. He preached the Good News that Christ lives his life in those who believe in him and that he blesses those who die trusting in him. For those who believe, Chrysostom said, "Death is a rest, a deliverance from the exhausting labors of this world. ... Think to whom the departed has gone—and take comfort." He confidently proclaimed the Good News that Jesus conquered death for us when he paid for our iniquities on the cross and rose from the dead.

In the year 398 John became bishop of Constantinople, which had become a high and powerful church office because Constantinople was then the capital of the empire. John started to reform both the church and the citizens as he preached sermons that spoke against the misuse of wealth by and the moral laxity of those in high places in the empire. Not everyone wanted to hear his call to renewed and disciplined Christian living. Urged by John's personal opponents, the emperor removed him from his office as bishop. But John's golden words did not stop.

Exiled for the rest of his life, John kept up his writing, encouraging Christians in beautiful and forceful words to live out their faith by maintaining high moral standards. As he was dying, his final words were, "Glory be to God for all things. Amen." His written legacy invites us to use the gifts God gives to the fullest. John Chrysostom's day on the church calendar of saints is observed by many Christians on January 27.

God of love, give us the gift of golden words. Let us speak only that which is right and truthful and helpful. Put the spirit of Jesus into our conversations to bless all who hear us. We ask this in his gracious name. Amen.

You might also want to pray for preachers and for those who are persecuted.

Justin Martyr
(c. 100–c. 165)

Explain Yourself

Always be prepared to give an answer to everyone who asks you to give the reason for the hope that you have. 1 Peter 3:15

Most great undertakings begin with one person: the trailblazer, the pioneer, the risk-taker who gets something done. In the history of the Christian church, Justin was the first apologist, that is, he first wrote down an explanation of Christian faith and worship practices, making them understandable to people who were not Christians, both friends and enemies.

Not that Justin necessarily seemed the most suitable candidate for the position. He was not born into a Christian family, nor was he a member of the clergy. He did not grow up in a center of the Christian faith. As is often the case with movers and shakers, he did not choose the job; instead, it found him. Justin sensed the need for the message of God's love in Jesus Christ to be shared, and, qualified or not, he devoted his life to speaking and writing about the Lord whom he had come to know. As a result, he grew into the job. That's still how it works with Christian witnesses. One needs only a readiness to tell about the grace of God through his Son, Jesus. No matter how or when any of us has come to faith, each of us has a story of faith and hope to share. God sees to that.

Justin was born around the year 100 at Flavia Neapolis, a Roman city north of Jerusalem. His family saw to it that he received a good classical education, including the study of many philosophies introduced by a variety of teachers. However, not until he met an old man who directed him to read the Scriptures did he find a faith to call his own. He wrote, "A flame was kindled in my soul; and a love of the prophets and of those men who are friends of Christ possessed me; and while revolving his words in my mind, I found this philosophy alone to be safe and profitable."

Justin was inspired both by the Christian message and by Christians he came to know, many of whom died as martyrs for the faith. Eventually Justin was counted among their number. On his second trip to Rome, where again he went to preach and teach the message of salvation through Christ, he was arrested and brought before the local magistrate. The public account of his trial and execution, accurately and historically kept by the Roman authorities, is the story of faith under fire. Summoned before the Roman prefect Rusticus, Justin refused to sacrifice to idols, affirming his Christian faith instead. The prefect questioned his beliefs saying, "So you think that you will go up to heaven, there to receive a reward?"

Justin calmly answered, "I don't think it; I know it. I have no doubt about it whatsoever."

Along with six other Christians, Justin was scourged and beheaded. Because of this, the title *Martyr* was added to his name, a badge of honor for this first apologist for Christ and the church. His day on the church calendar is usually observed on April 14.

Inspire us as your witnesses, Lord. Give us opportunities and words to express the hope of Christ that is in us. Keep alive our vision of heaven, while we live to your glory on earth. We ask this in Jesus' name. Amen.

You may also want to pray for theologians and defenders of the faith.

Saint Katherine
(c. 287–c. 307)

Young and Faith-Full

Don't let anyone look down on you because you are young, but set an example for the believers in life, in love, in faith and in purity. 1 Timothy 4:12

Do you have a favorite saint? Many people do. One of the favorite saints of people living in the earliest Christian centuries was Katherine, an Egyptian girl who died for her faith while still quite young. In the years after her death, Katherine became such a favorite that numerous notable churches and monasteries were named in her honor all over the ancient world. The church next to the traditional site of Jesus' birth is named for Saint Katherine, as is the monastery at the top of Mount Sinai, where Moses received the Ten Commandments from God. Katherine, the beautiful girl who suffered a martyr's death at an early age, has been a favorite saint for centuries.

Although historical traditions about this young witness to Christ vary, her story is compelling. Katherine was born into a wealthy family in the large and cultured city of Alexandria in northern Egypt as the third century after Christ was closing. An outstanding student, she read extensively in the areas of philosophy and religion. Through her reading of the Bible for one of her classes, she discovered the Christian faith. The amazing love of God, who gave his one and only Son to save the world, spoke to her heart. The Holy Spirit called her to believe in Jesus. Katherine became a Christian and was baptized.

Although probably still in her teens, she witnessed to the truth of salvation through Jesus Christ, which put her life in jeopardy. What turned out to be the final Roman state persecution of Christians under the Emperor Maxentius had recently begun. Courageously, Katherine went before the pagan emperor, asking that the persecutions stop. He responded by ordering her to give up her faith. Katherine firmly refused to deny her Lord Jesus. Impressed by her intelligence and youthful beauty, the emperor invited the young woman to come and live with him. When she turned him down, he had her thrown into prison.

Even in captivity, Katherine witnessed to her faith with amazing results. In the months after her Baptism, she had converted 50 philosophers who had come to argue her out of her beliefs. Continuing her Gospel witness from her jail cell, Katherine talked constantly about her faith in Christ. That fearless witness resulted in the conversion of not only the empress, who had come to visit her, but also of 200 soldiers sent to guard her.

Katherine touched the hearts and lives of hundreds of people before she was executed. Even through her last hours, she radiated the love of Jesus, who suffered death for her sake and our sakes. A final tradition about Katherine relates she was still such a favorite saint six centuries after her martyrdom that, around the year 900, her remains were taken to the chapel on Mount Sinai named in her honor. "Be faithful, even to the point of death," Saint John encouraged his readers in the book of Revelation (2:10). Katherine of Alexandria was, and we remember her on November 25.

Eternal Lord, inspire us to faithfulness in all ages of our lives. Whether our span of days is short or long, may we, through the indwelling of the Holy Spirit, glorify you with our words and our deeds. We pray in Jesus' powerful name. Amen.

You may also want to pray for children and young people and for boldness to witness to the faith.

Saint Laurence
(c. 220–258)

The True Wealth of People

God chose the foolish things of the world to shame the wise; God chose the weak things of the world to shame the strong. 1 Corinthians 1:27

Having a sense of humor can be a blessing in many situations, even deadly ones. The martyr with a smile, Laurence lived and died during the reign of Valerian, one of the last Roman emperors to persecute Christians.

Born in Spain, Laurence, also spelled Lawrence, found his way to Rome, where he served in the church as a deacon doing many of the same things deacons do today—caring for the social and physical needs of people. At Laurence's time, the churches in Rome cared for more than 1500 poor people and sent contributions to other parts of the empire. As a deacon, Laurence assisted in distributing these gifts.

In 258 a severe persecution of Christians began in Rome. Sixtus, the bishop, was executed. Hoping to make financial gain for the city from the bishop's death, the Roman prefect in office demanded that deacon Laurence bring him all the wealth of the church within three days. With a sense of holy humor, Laurence showed up before the prefect right on time three days later, but with no silver or gold. He brought people instead. He filled the city courtyard with thousands of people: poor, blind and sick, widows and elderly. Surrounded by them, he stood before the prefect and exclaimed, "The church is truly rich, far richer than your emperor." Laurence knew that in God's economy, people are of far greater value than things. God cared so much about sinful people that he sent his Son Jesus to bring us salvation and the promise of eternal life. We can smile in any situation because we know of God's great love for each of us.

Laurence kept his sense of humor until the end of his life, which came abruptly. The prefect of Rome was so upset with the presentation of the "true riches of the church" that he ordered a slow death on a gridiron for the deacon. Having been placed over the glowing fire on one side, with a smile Laurence said to the executioner, "Let my body be turned; one side is broiled enough." Laurence kept the faith and, as Martin Luther observed, "overcame death and all tortures." His faithfulness, his care for the poor, and his sense of humor are an inspiration for every age. Laurence's day on the calendar of saints is August 10.

Bless us with saint-like natures, Lord. May we be known as people who have a regard for things holy and a sense of things humorous. This we ask through Jesus Christ, our Savior. Amen.

You may also want to pray for an increased concern for people, especially the unemployed and the needy.

Saint Margaret
(1045–1093)

A Mother's Legacy

A wife of noble character who can find? She is worth far more than rubies. … Her children arise and call her blessed; her husband also, and he praises her: "Many women do noble things, but you surpass them all." Proverbs 31:10, 28–29

Some people's lives positively affect their neighborhood, their town, or their state. Margaret's life blessed the whole nation of Scotland—not only while she lived, but for centuries to follow. She brought love for culture and the arts, charity, and Christian piety to the far northern reaches of Europe, traditions carried on by her descendants long after her death in 1093.

Margaret's family tree was full of royalty. Her father was an English prince in exile, her mother a German princess living in the court of Hungary. Before she had reached her teens, Margaret was sent to the court of England, where she lived until the Battle of Hastings in 1066, when she became an exile. Finding refuge with old family friends, Margaret arrived at the court of the Scottish King Malcolm, who became infatuated with her beauty and her gracious ways. After an extended courtship, the couple was married at Dunfermline in 1070. Margaret was now a queen.

Scotland in the Middle Ages was famous for its wild and brawling ways. People had little education and knew little about the Christian faith. The church in Scotland was corrupt and chaotic. But that changed once Margaret ascended to the throne. She supported those who opposed the selling of church offices. She set regulations for marriage and standardized Christian feasts and the calendar of the church. Margaret's faith in Jesus as the Lord of her life reached from the great affairs of the Scottish nation, which she directed with her husband, to the small details of daily life in the castle. At her invitation, groups of women even met together to study Scripture and embroider church vestments and altar cloths. In a sense, Queen Margaret was the founder of the altar guilds that serve in our churches.

Finding what we can do to the glory of God challenges each of us, as it did Margaret. Jesus Christ died for all, bringing us forgiveness of sins and the promise of eternal life. The life of faith that we live and the legacy of faith we leave behind are important expressions of our response to God's goodness in Christ.

Perhaps Margaret's greatest legacy came through her children, six sons and two daughters, whom she raised with careful Christian guidance. One of her biographers writes, "Her children surpassed in good behavior many who were their elders; they were always affectionate and peaceable among themselves." On her deathbed she requested this of the castle chaplain: "That you assist my children and teach them to fear and love God."

The description of the ideal wife written in the final chapter of Proverbs fits her most comfortably. Her children, a number of whom became rulers in their generation, continued her concern for Christian charity. Margaret's day on the church calendar is November 16.

Spirit of God, direct us in ways by which we leave a heritage of blessing. Beginning with our daily lives of home and family, show us how to live for him who loved us and gave himself for us. We ask this in his wonderful name. Amen.

You might also want to pray for mothers and families and for altar guilds.

Saint Martin
(c. 316–c. 397)

A Cloak of Righteousness

But you, man of God, flee from all this, and pursue righteousness, godliness, faith, love, endurance and gentleness. Fight the good fight of the faith. 1 Timothy 6:11–12

"Choose your battles wisely," says an old proverb. Martin of Tours did that. Beginning his adult life as a cavalry soldier for Rome, he concluded it as a soldier for Jesus Christ who bravely fought the good fight of the faith. Instead of battling enemy soldiers from his horse, Martin, an ordained exorcist, battled evil spirits. Traveling on his donkey and by foot, he spread the Good News about Jesus the Savior throughout unevangelized areas of what is now France, earning the nickname "Glory to Gaul."

Martin was born into a pagan family in the Roman province of Upper Pannonia (now Hungary). The son of a military officer, Martin was expected to choose the same career. Although he had been introduced to the Christian faith around the age of 10, the teenage Martin enlisted in the legions of Rome, planning to be a career soldier. But God had other plans for him—as he has plans for each of us. Saint Paul writes to the Ephesians that God "made known to us the mystery of his will according to his good pleasure, which he purposed in Christ" (Ephesians 1:9). With Christ in our lives, the door of our destiny opens. As the center of our lives, God blesses us with his power, a power that often brings changes. For Martin that life-changing power took hold of him when he was 18.

One winter day, Martin's regiment came to Amiens (now in France). By the city gate was a beggar, shivering from the cold. The Roman procession passed him by—except for Martin. The young soldier on horseback stopped for a moment, took out his sword, cut his military cloak *(capa)* into two pieces, and gave half to the needy man. "It is all I have to give; I have no money," he said as he rode off to rejoin his legion. Shortly after, in a vision, Martin recognized Christ in the face of the beggar whom he had aided. Martin's life was changed—and so was his vocation. "I am Christ's soldier; I am not allowed to fight," he said as he left military service to become a hermit, a monk living by himself. Immediately he was baptized in the name of Christ and began a solitary religious life of prayer and contemplation. In his way, Martin was a Christian pacifist, joining a long tradition of people who have felt directed by their faith not to engage in warfare. (Of interest, it was Martin's own *capa* that stands behind the word *chaplain*.)

Martin's career as a solitary monk did not last long. God had still other plans for him. Using his many talents, Martin established churches and abbeys through-out Gaul and, in about 371, was consecrated bishop of Tours, an office he held until his death. Because of his long and dedicated service to Christ, Martin became one of the first nonmartyrs included on the calendar of saints, being remembered on November 11. In his honor, Martin's name has been given to many shrines, churches, and people, including Martin Luther, who was baptized on the 11th of November 1483.

Change us and shape our lives to reflect our faith, Lord. As soldiers of Christ, give us opportunities to share what we have and what we believe. In Jesus' name we ask this. Amen.

You might also want to pray for the armed forces and their chaplains.

Michael

The Archangel of Might

At that time Michael, the great prince who protects your people, will arise. Daniel 12:1

Uncounted millions of angels serve God and his people. Scripture refers to an organization of celestial beings, something like a massive army. Although Scripture does not discuss the ranks of angels, we can assume that archangels are over angels. One of the few individuals named in these countless legions is Michael, an archangel written of in the Old and the New Testaments. Michael, whose name means "who is like God?" is one of the mightiest of the angels of God, all of whom possess great and glorious power.

The Old Testament book of Daniel identifies Michael as the protector of God's people (Daniel 10:21; 12:1). The New Testament book of Jude (v. 9) tells of Michael contending with the devil himself, and the book of Revelation (12:7) shows him leading the heavenly host to a great final victory over Satan and the forces of darkness. How good to have Michael on your side!

Michael, along with all other angels, has yet another task: he will accompany Jesus at his second coming. An archangel, perhaps Michael, will herald the return of the victorious Lord. Saint Paul writes to the Thessalonians of that glorious day, "For the Lord himself will come down from heaven, with a loud command, with the voice of the archangel and with the trumpet call of God, and the dead in Christ will rise first" (1 Thessalonians 4:16). God promises that whoever believes in Jesus, our Savior from sin, will see that great appearing—which may not be that far off.

Michael's activities have received much attention in writings and legends through the centuries. A document titled "Words of the Book of Michael Rehearsed unto the Angels" was found among the Dead Sea documents a few decades ago. As the one who leads the faithful to the harbor of heaven, he is featured in the well-known folk song "Michael, Row the Boat Ashore."

September 29, the festival day of Michael and all angels, has been on the calendar since the fifth century. In England that date still marks the opening of the autumn court session and the beginning of the fall semester at the Universities of Cambridge and Oxford.

God of all creation, we thank you for all the company of heaven. Let your holy angels ever be with us, to defend and protect us. We ask this in Jesus' name. Amen.

You may also want to pray for the safety and encouragement of church leaders.

Saint Monica
(c. 331–387)

A Mother's Love

Be joyful always; pray continually; give thanks in all circumstances, for this is God's will for you in Christ Jesus.
1 Thessalonians 5:16–18

There are no typical saints. Monica proves that point. You might picture the average saint as a tall, pale-skinned, European holy man, with a patient and placid temperament. Monica was a tiny, dark-skinned African woman, with grim determination and ready tears. She meddled in her children's lives and seemed to wear out her welcome wherever she went. But in God's economy her liabilities became assets.

Monica had many personal obstacles to overcome in her life. Born in North Africa to Christian parents near the start of the fourth century, she was married off at an early age to a pagan named Patricius. Marriage at that time was often much less than a partnership; wives often found themselves cheated on, beaten, or deserted. But Monica held to her faith and her hopes, living a life of devotion and dedication to her family. Shortly before his death, her husband converted to the Christian faith—as did his mother, who had been less than charitable to Monica for many years. Needless to say, Monica rejoiced.

If being a Christian wife challenged Monica, being a Christian mother, especially to her oldest son, Augustine, proved a greater challenge. His behavior so completely clashed with her Christian ideals that for some time she refused to let him into the family home. Yet she always kept praying that he would find in Jesus Christ a true direction for his life. When she confided her hopes and her sorrows to her bishop he said, "It is not possible that a son of so many tears should be lost." Monica's life testifies to the value of prayer to God, who hears our prayers and concerns, no matter how difficult the situation.

Monica's prayers for her son received a ready answer. Wanting to leave Africa behind, Augustine set off for Italy where he became a teacher, first in Rome and then in Milan. Shadowing his every move and tracing the path with her prayers, Monica followed him across the Mediterranean Sea and set up housekeeping for him, evicting the woman he had lived with for many years (and the mother of his son). After a special encounter with God's Word, Augustine's life turned around. He and his son were baptized at Milan in 387. (His many years of service to Christ as a hero of the early church were just beginning. He would become the church's great proclaimer of forgiveness of sins through Jesus Christ alone.) (See "Saint Augustine.")

With Augustine's life now devoted to the Lord, Monica felt that her mission on earth was accomplished. She died in Italy that same year, never again seeing her native Africa. This pushy and manipulative mother brought blessing not only to her family but to the many people who were strengthened in faith by the writings of her gifted son. Many remember Monica, a most untypical yet believable saint, on May 4.

Make me a saint in your service, Lord. I know that I have my weaknesses and my faults, and yet I pray that I can bring you glory somehow. Direct my life, and help me to rejoice in living for you. This I ask in the name of Jesus, the great forgiver. Amen.

You may also want to pray for parents and grandparents.

Saint Nicholas
(c. 275–c. 342)

A Creative Giver

I know your deeds, your love and faith, your service and perseverance. Revelation 2:19

Saint John wrote the above words to the church at Thyatira in Asia Minor, but they could well have been spoken personally to Saint Nicholas, who lived in that same area a few centuries later. To this day the church remembers his deeds of charity and giving. Every year the tradition of Santa Claus expands on his acts of kindness and love.

Not much of Nicholas' personal history is known, except that he served as bishop at Myra, a city in Asia Minor (now Turkey), in the fourth century and that he is remembered for being both generous and selfless. Left a wealthy orphan at a young age, he used his inheritance to help people in need. Like Christians in our time who have followed that pattern of charity, he found satisfaction in giving to others.

The most famous story told about Nicholas has three happy endings. In the town of Myra, a very poor man had three daughters of marriageable age. Because they had no dowry money for any young man who might want to marry them, the girls anticipated lives as spinsters or even prostitutes. One night a bag of gold was thrown into the room where the three girls slept. The oldest daughter used the money for her dowry and married well. Soon after, another nighttime bag of gold came through the girls' bedroom window, and the middle daughter also married prosperously. When a third bag of gold was thrown through the window for the final daughter, the father discovered Nicholas providing the dowry money. He was overwhelmed by the kindness of the generous bishop.

The name of Saint Nicholas soon became associated with giving special gifts. Through the Dutch settlers of New Amsterdam, who remembered the bishop as Sinter Klaas, the legend came to America, where Santa Claus still is known as the kind bringer of gifts.

Devoted to charity, Nicholas was also dedicated to doctrine. According to some writers, he attended the Council of Nicaea and spoke on behalf of orthodox Christian teaching and against the heresies of that era. Imprisoned during the time of persecution ordered by Emperor Diocletian of Rome, he witnessed boldly to his faith in Jesus. Every account about Nicholas describes a likable and benevolent man who found life's riches in Jesus, the Savior from sin. Nicholas used his wealth and all of his life as an offering of thanks to God. Although his church calendar day is December 6, "jolly old Saint Nicholas" is an example for us every day of the year.

Gracious Lord, may we be more than informed or even impressed by the lives of your saints of centuries past. Today may they inspire us to deeds of love and faith, to service and perseverance. For Jesus' sake. Amen.

You may also want to pray for a rich measure of generosity.

Saint Patrick
(c. 389–c. 461)

Beyond the Legends

I will also make you a light for the Gentiles, that you may bring my salvation to the ends of the earth. Isaiah 49:6

Shelves of bookstores today seem to be overloaded with autobiographies. Everyone wants to tell the story of his or her life down to the last detail. A few of these books are interesting; most are not. Few saints on the church calendar have written autobiographies. Patrick is a singular exception. In his *Confessio*, he relates the story of his amazing life and tells about his mission work in Ireland. With great humility he writes, "I, Patrick, a sinner, am the most ignorant and of least account of the faithful, despised by many. ... I owe it to God's grace that so many people should through me be born again to him."

Patrick was born into a Christian family living along the west coast of England during a time when the Roman Empire was losing its control of Britain. What had been a safe place during his childhood became dangerous as Patrick entered his teen years. At the age of 16, he was seized as a slave by coastal raiders and taken to Ireland, a harsh and mostly pagan place. For six years he was kept as a forced worker, sustained by the Christian faith he had learned from his father, a deacon, and from his grandfather, a priest. Patrick wrote: "Now after I came to Ireland, daily I pastured flocks, and constantly during the day I prayed." One of Patrick's many answered prayers came in the form of a ship on which he escaped to France. After a time of studying in monasteries there, he returned to his home in England. But the spiritual needs of the Irish people never left his mind and his heart. He knew he had a mission for the Lord to complete.

Patrick did not immediately go back to the Emerald Isle, but rather prepared for his return through study and prayer. In 432, Patrick, now a middle-aged bishop, stepped again on the shore of the land of his captivity. It was a fearsome place for a Christian missionary, with warring tribal chieftains and hostile Druid priests everywhere. Undeterred, Patrick went fearlessly throughout the island, preaching Christ and founding monasteries, churches, and schools. Fully aware of the dangers at hand, he wrote in his notebook, "Daily I expect either a violent death, or a return to slavery, or some other calamity. ... I have cast myself into the hands of Almighty God, for he rules everything."

The great calamities Patrick anticipated never happened. During his long and productive life, most of Ireland came to receive the Christian faith. His written legacy includes not only the autobiographical *Confessio* but other correspondence and hymns, including the famous "breastplate" hymn that begins "I bind unto myself today the strong name of the Trinity."

Patrick believed in the power of God and in the saving work of Jesus Christ, our Lord. He wrote, "For beyond all doubt we shall rise on that day in the crystal brightness of the sun; that is, in the glory of Christ Jesus our Redeemer." Patrick, whose traditional symbols are the snake and the shamrock, is remembered by the church on March 17. Among his prayers is this invocation:

High King of heaven, may your strength ever guide us, your might sustain us, your wisdom direct us, your eye look before us, your ear listen to us, your Word speak for us, and your hand protect us today and forever. In Jesus' name we ask it. Amen.

You might also want to pray for missionaries and for the church in Ireland.

Saint Polycarp
(c. 69–c. 156)

Practice What You Preach

To the angel of the church in Smyrna write: ... Do not be afraid of what you are about to suffer. Revelation 2:8, 10

Polycarp is a golden link in the chain of saints. He joins the era of the disciples and apostles to the time of the great Christian writers and leaders of the second century. As a young man, Polycarp personally knew the apostle John, Jesus' beloved disciple, and studied under him. His writings as bishop of Smyrna frequently quote the books of the New Testament we know (for example, 1 Peter and 1 John). Polycarp took what he had received and passed it on faithfully to the next generation.

A committed believer in Jesus as Lord, Polycarp governed the church at Smyrna (now in Turkey) for over half a century. Many Christians became martyrs by being executed for their faith in Jesus Christ during those years, including Polycarp himself. In his epistle to the Philippians, he had written that Christian martyrs should serve as examples to the faithful. His own opportunity came when he was arrested during the rule of the Emperor Marcus Aurelius. Polycarp's captors took him to the local stadium where he was commanded to renounce his faith. When the governor ordered, "Curse Christ," Polycarp replied, "Eighty and six years have I served him, and he has done me no wrong, and can I revile my king that saved me?"

The detailed account of Polycarp's trial, his example of faith, and his execution circulated widely throughout the early church. One witness noted that, when he was being burned alive, "he looked, not like burning flesh, but like bread in the oven or gold and silver being refined in a furnace." The date of his death, which is still widely observed, is the first recorded commemoration of a martyr. Polycarp had lived out the call to suffering that his teacher John had recorded in the book of Revelation, exemplifying the well-known verse "Blessed are the dead who die in the Lord from now on. … They will rest from their labor, for their deeds will follow them" (Revelation 14:13).

Polycarp is not a name we hear frequently. Translated from the Greek, it means "much fruit." In John's gospel we have the promise of Jesus that "if a man remains in me and I in him, he will bear much fruit; apart from me you can do nothing" (John 15:5). Polycarp's fruitful life witnessed to God's faithfulness in keeping his promises. That example of lifelong fruitfulness is still remembered.

Polycarp did not die alone. A number of younger people who had learned from him about salvation and heaven followed him to martyrs' deaths. Their number continues to grow even in our time, as in some places in the world people still choose being true to their faith over their earthly lives. We can thank God for the special witness of "the noble army of martyrs" as we remember Polycarp on February 23.

Holy Spirit, make us fruitful in our times and places. When people insult or threaten us for following Jesus, keep us strong and steady, entrusting ourselves to him who bore our sin in his body on the tree of the cross. Bless our good confession of you, who with the Father and the Son are one God forever. Amen.

You may also want to pray for boldness to witness to Jesus and for those who suffer for their confession of Christ.

Saint Radegund
(518–587)

Doing Whatever It Takes

Each one should use whatever gift he has received to serve others, faithfully administering God's grace in its various forms. 1 Peter 4:10

Radegund was a comfortable saint, the kind with whom you might like to spend an afternoon in the bustling French nunnery she directed. She had the gift of hospitality, which she used frequently and creatively. Putting into practice Christian charity, she was able to cope with difficulties, turning them into blessings throughout her lifetime.

Europe in the sixth century was a battleground. Kings, dukes, counts, and other nobles constantly fought over land and possessions. Born in Erfurt (Germany), Radegund began life as a Thuringian princess. When she was 12, however, her pagan father was murdered by his brother, who subsequently was defeated in battle by Clothaire, a Frankish king. This rough-edged ruler took Radegund as a captive to his castle in

France. There she received a good education and religious instruction from Christian teachers. After six years, Clothaire the king married her, much against her wishes.

Trying to make the best of an unpleasant situation, Radegund devoted her time to caring for captives in the castle as well as for the area's poor and sick. Although she was not happily married, she remained true to her wedding vows—until her husband murdered her brother. Summoning up her courage, she left the royal fortress and went to the local bishop, asking to become a deaconess of the church. By taking religious vows, she could be released from her marriage contract. Surprisingly, Clothaire agreed to his wife's decision and gave her a family estate at Saix. There she established a center for charity, which included care for lepers. Radegund believed in hands-on hospitality. She did everything from scrubbing floors to cleaning toilets, both at Saix and later at the abbey of Poitiers, which she filled with over 200 nuns, whom she supervised and directed.

Radegund's faith in Jesus kept her going and growing. Under her leadership, the abbey became a world-famous center for education, literature, and the arts. Encouraging poets, writers, and musicians, she extended hospitality to many singers, including a musician named Venantius Fortunatus, who had traveled to France from his native Italy. Fortunatus became chaplain of the abbey and the composer of many hymns. Some of these, such as "The Royal Banners Forward Go" and "Hail Thee, Festival Day," are still being sung in the church.

Caring about situations beyond the abbey walls, Radegund wrote to national leaders, seeking peaceful resolutions to the wars and conflicts that continually raged throughout Europe. Despite her busy schedule, her personal life included extensive time for devotion and prayer. In many ways she became a counterpart of Saint Paul, who had once written to the Philippians, "I have learned the secret of being content in any and every situation. ... I can do everything through him who gives me strength" (4:12–13). She knew Jesus' forgiving and loving presence in her life, as do his followers today.

In the year 587, Radegund died, having extended hospitality in the name of Christ to beggars, kings, and everyone in between. Her day on the calendar of the church is August 13.

Stir up in us the gift of hospitality and of service to those around us, Lord. Show us how to find contentment in our daily lives and how to use every occasion to bring glory to your name. We ask this for Jesus' sake. Amen.

You may also want to pray for peacemakers.

Raphael

The Angel of Healing

For he will command his angels concerning you to guard you in all your ways. Psalm 91:11

Guardian angels are of special interest these days. Many accounts have been given by people who are certain that at a crucial time in their lives, an angel intervened to get them out of a tough situation. Stories about guardian angels often have themes and even details in common. First in the long line of guardian angel accounts is the appearance of Raphael, the angel of healing. He appears as a main character in the book of Tobit, one of the books of the Apocrypha, a collection of literature from the centuries immediately preceding the birth of Jesus.

The book of Tobit tells a tale about the importance of prayer and faithful living. In his commentary on this story, Martin Luther observed, "This book is good and useful for us Christians to read. It is the work of a fine Hebrew author who deals not with trivial but important issues, and whose writings and concerns are extraordinarily Christian." Angels are of more than passing interest to Christians of every age.

In the book of Tobit we meet Raphael, a guardian angel sent to accompany a young man named Tobias, the son of Tobit, on a journey far from his home. Tobias thinks that his companion is merely a guide who knows the trade routes through Persia; the reader knows much more. The fact that Tobias and his family don't know Raphael's true identity adds suspense to this story, which is filled with demons and treasure and narrow escapes. Not until the end of the journey, when Tobias, his new bride, and his fortune have returned to the aged Tobit and his wife, is Raphael's true identity discovered by everyone in the tale. But then that is the way it often is with guardian angels— we just don't always recognize them.

God does things in his way and in his good time. It was in God's good time that Jesus came to earth to suffer and die for us to win our salvation. Throughout his time on earth angels ministered to Jesus. Among them may well have been Raphael.

Raphael has the reputation for being concerned both with people who travel and with those who are ill. In the book of Tobit he guards both Tobias and his dog throughout their travels and, at the close of the story, heals Tobit from his blindness. Frequently in artistic representations, Raphael is shown with sandals, a water gourd, and a wallet as well as with his trusty walking stick. A friendly angel, he enjoys the work God has given him.

In Psalm 91, we are reminded that God has appointed many guardian angels with the responsibility of watching out for us year after year. Whether we are young or old, married or single, God has promised us the care of guardian angels. Part of our adventure of life as God's people is to be on the lookout for angels in disguise, realizing that, along with blessings and care, God often sends surprises.

Gracious Lord, you bring protection and healing to us in many ways. Help us to sense the presence of your holy angels as we travel on our pilgrimage through life. In Jesus' name. Amen.

You may also want to pray for the safety of travelers and give thanks for the presence of guardian angels.

Saint Sergius
(c. 1315–c. 1392)

Clothes Do Not Make the Man

And what does the LORD require of you? To act justly and to love mercy and to walk humbly with your God. Micah 6:8

Clothes do not always make the man. One of the most influential figures in Russian history, Sergius of Radonezh, dressed throughout his adult life like a peasant. When offered the golden robes that went with being the primate of Moscow, the highest church office in his land, he replied, "Since the days of my youth I have never worn gold. Now that I am an old man, more than ever I adhere to my poverty." Even at the height of his fame and power, when he was consulted by princes and other rulers, Sergius continued to wear patched clothes and old felt boots.

Sergius had not been born poor. His noble family, who lived near Rostov, had him baptized Bartholomew and raised him with education and culture. His comfortable world was shattered when he was 15. Driven from their estate in a civil war, his parents became peasant farmers near Moscow. When they died, Bartholomew, who now was 20, and his brother Stephen chose to leave the confusion and unrest they found in the world around them by taking up the isolated lives of religious hermits, building a log cabin and small chapel for themselves deep in the Russian forest. After a severe winter, Stephen decided to join a monastery. Bartholomew, who had now taken the monastic name Sergius, stayed on alone at the retreat in the dark and lonely woods. Silence, something in short supply in our bustling and noise-filled world, brought him a special closeness to God.

Sergius' lifestyle of prayer and simplicity attracted many followers. Soon he had organized 40 communities for Christian study and reflection. Still he took time for silent meditation and daily work in the monastery garden. Sergius helped many men and women meditate on the presence of God in their lives through the experience of contemplative prayer. They saw working in him the Holy Spirit, vital and active.

For Sergius, faith combined prayer with action. When Prince Dimitri of Moscow consulted him about fighting the Muslim Tatars, Sergius took an icon (a religious picture) and led the soldiers toward the battle, which preserved Christianity in Russia. In his later years he traveled widely, establishing peace among rival princes. Honored as a *starets* (wise elder), he stopped civil wars and improved the lives of people in 14th-century Russia. In deeds of justice and mercy, he reflected the great mercy of God shown to all people in Jesus

Christ, the one who paid for our salvation not with gold or silver, but with his blood on the cross. We are clothed with his righteousness, no matter what our personal wardrobe might be.

Sergius, finishing his life in his traditional simple threads, died at one of the monasteries he had established. We can thank God for the example of Sergius, who, by linking prayer with action, brought God's blessing to the Russian people. His day on the church calendar is September 25.

Grant us grace, dear Lord, to act justly, to love mercy, and to walk humbly with you throughout our lives. In Jesus' name. Amen.

You may also want to pray for the church in Russia and for Christian artists and artisans.

Thomas Aquinas
(c. 1225–1274)

Work and Pray; Pray and Work

Never be lacking in zeal, but keep your spiritual fervor, serving the Lord. Be joyful in hope, patient in affliction, faithful in prayer. Romans 12:11–12

Many of the prayers that we use in our worship have unique histories. Someone, somewhere, at some time first put the thought into words and then the words into writing. Although hymn writers are acknowledged by name in our hymnals, prayer writers generally are not.

Thomas Aquinas is the writer of the traditional Collect for Maundy Thursday, a prayer that focuses not only on the meaning but also on the result of Holy Communion. The high regard in which Aquinas held the Lord's Supper is found in his words of prayer: "O Lord Jesus, since you have left us a memorial of your Passion in a wonderful sacrament, grant, we pray, that we may so use this sacrament of your body and blood that the fruits of your redeeming work may continually be manifest in us."

The fruits of the redeeming work of Christ were obvious in the life of Thomas from his earliest years. Born in the castle of his noble Italian family, he renounced his family's secular plans for his life and became a monk, totally devoted to teaching, to preaching, and to prayer. Years of study took him from Italy to Cologne, Germany, where he became a pupil of Albertus Magnus, a noted church scholar. He completed his theological doctorate at the University of Paris and became part of the faculty as a popular teacher and lecturer.

Along with fame and recognition, Thomas' way with words earned him the nickname "the Angelic Doctor." Throughout his extensive writing career, Thomas never forgot the source of his ability. Frequently in the margins of his works he would write, "I pray to you, Lord, or I am lost." Being in prayer contact with God was at the heart of his labor; it was said that "his wonderful learning owes far less to his genius than to the effectiveness of his prayer."

In his life of prayer, Thomas Aquinas offers us a devotional model. Through our prayers, we call upon Jesus, our Lord and our Brother, who gave his life for us. Reflecting on prayers written for us by men and women of faith from generations past, we are able to learn from models of devotion to Christ which help us to grow in the exercise of our own faith. In his final years, Thomas set aside paper and pen and increased his time for prayer and contemplation, stating, "All that I have written appears to be as so much straw after the things that have been revealed to me." Thomas died at the age of 48 while traveling to a church council at Lyons, France. His literary works, including the massive *Summa Theologica*, continue to be studied today. Thomas from Aquino is generally remembered on March 7.

Let our prayers be faithful and frequent and fervent, Lord. May our devotional lives use the best of our time, our thoughts, and our language for you. We ask this humbly in the name of Jesus, our Savior and our Friend. Amen.

You may also want to pray for seminaries and Christian colleges and for teachers of theology.

Uriel

The Angel of Light

In speaking of the angels he says, "He makes his angels winds, his servants flames of fire." Hebrews 1:7

Although we can get to know many saints by name and personality, we can't do the same with angels. Actually, the Bible mentions only two angels by name: Michael and Gabriel. Other literature from Bible times acquaints us with two additional angels, Uriel and Raphael. According to the book of Enoch (9:1), these four angels surround the throne of heaven. Enoch is a book of the pseudepigrapha, works attributed to Old Testament figures but not included in the Bible and written between 200 B.C. and A.D. 200.

The name Uriel means "fire of God," and frequently this angel is associated with biblical accounts of fire and catastrophe. According to tradition, Uriel was the angel that God placed at the gate of the Garden of Eden with the flaming sword flashing back and forth to guard the way to the tree of life (Genesis 3:24). It was Uriel who echoed God's message warning Noah about the coming flood, so that he set about the difficult task of building the ark. Uriel became both the messenger of retribution and a force behind the deluge. Both in the book of Psalms and in the letter to the Hebrews, we read that God "makes his angels winds, his servants flames of fire" (Hebrews 1:7; Psalm 104:4).

Books and articles about angels are popular these days. Some stress the traditional view that angels are personalized spirits with specific heavenly duties. Martin Luther reflected this perspective in his definition: "An angel is a spiritual creature, a personal being without a body, appointed for the service of the divine church." Angels get things done for God. Appearing in many forms, they often complete their assignments totally unnoticed by the people they are assisting.

The writer of Hebrews, in chapter 1, points out that Jesus, the Son of God, is superior to the angels. Angels have their places and their powers, but it is Jesus, God in the flesh, who possesses the power to forgive sins and to grant everlasting life. Because of Jesus, we joyfully await the time in heaven when we will meet the angels and even get to know a few more of them by name.

***

God of earth and of heaven, we thank you for the ministry of the angels. Give us eyes to see you working through them and grant us at last the heavenly vision of the angelic host around your eternal throne. We ask this for Jesus' sake. Amen.

You may also want to pray that the Lord will give his guardian angels charge over you and your loved ones.

Saint Valentine
(c. 222–270)

The Sign of God's Love

Love the LORD, *all his saints! … Be strong and take heart, all you who hope in the* LORD. Psalm 31:23–24

Saint Valentine's Day is the one saint's day that just about everyone in North America and throughout much of Europe celebrates. Yet almost nobody seems to know why. Cutout hearts, colorful greetings, and bright red decorations enliven the middle of February—all because of a martyr from the third century, about whom very little is known. As with the lives of many saints, what history cannot tell us about Valentine, legend fills in.

A physician and priest in Rome during the rule of Emperor Claudius, Valentine lived in a time when Christians were being harshly persecuted because of their religion. Arrested for his Christian faith, he received a death sentence from the Roman authorities. While he was waiting in prison for the executioner's ax, Valentine developed a friendship with the young daughter of his jailer. He told the girl about Jesus and his hope of heaven. On the day of his execution, he left her a note cut into a special shape. Written inside was a message of affection and encouragement. He signed the letter "your Valentine," beginning a singular tradition.

The story of Valentine's greeting grew through the centuries as pagan practices were given Christian associations. As an adaptation of the Roman Lupercalia festival held each year to celebrate the first signs of spring, the day of Saint Valentine became an annual occurrence. By the Middle Ages, the 14th of February, thought to be the day on which birds chose their mates, was well established as a special time for writing love letters and sending romantic gifts. The custom continues around the world today.

Expressing love is what the Valentine's Day observance is all about. But as Christians, we celebrate a love far richer than the usual fluff of February 14. Centuries ago the psalmist wrote, "Love the LORD, all his saints" (Psalm 31:23). We have good reason to express love for the Lord. Saint John writes, "We love because he first loved us" (1 John 4:19). God showed his love through the death of Jesus Christ for our sins, giving us the lasting sign of his love and the reason to show love toward him and to one another.

Love for God and the hope of heaven enabled Valentine to "take heart" and face his own death as a martyr. He left behind a greeting to a young girl, a testimony of faith, and a lasting example of love and caring in Jesus' name. February 14 is special on the calendar because each year it reminds us of the genuine love and the moving witness of Valentine, an ancient and faithful saint.

Lord of love, bless our remembering of the saints of ages past. Help us proclaim your love in our day in word and deed as we look forward to the great reunion of all the saints in heaven. In Jesus' name. Amen.

You might also want to pray for your loved ones.

Appendix

A Chronology of Saints
(Dates arranged according to year of death.)

Saints from the First Christian Centuries: A.D. 100–300

Clement c. 35–c. 100

Ignatius c. 40–117

Polycarp c. 69–c. 156

Justin Martyr c. 100–c. 165

Cecelia c. 214–c. 230

Hippolytus c. 170–c. 236

Laurence c. 220–258

Valentine c. 222–270

Saints from the Early Church: A.D. 300–400

Katherine c. 287–c. 307

Helena c. 255–c. 329

Nicholas c. 275–c. 342

Hilary c. 310–368

Athanasius c. 295–373

Basil 329–379

Monica c. 331–387

Martin c. 316–c. 397

Ambrose 340–397

Saints from the Expanding Church: A.D. 400–800

John Chrysostom c. 347–407

Jerome c. 345–420

Augustine 354–430

Patrick c. 389–c. 461

Benedict 480–543

Radegund 518–587

Columba c. 521–597

Gregory c. 540–604

Hilda 614–680

Boniface c. 673–c. 754

Saints from the Middle Ages: A.D. 800–1400

Ansgar 801–865

Margaret 1045–1093

Anselm 1033–1109

Bernard 1090–1153

Francis of Assisi c. 1181–1226

Elizabeth c. 1207–1231

Thomas Aquinas c. 1225–1274

Bridget 1303–1373

Sergius c. 1315–c. 1392

A Calendar of Saints and Angels*

January

2 Basil

13 Hilary

27 John Chrysostom

February

3 Ansgar

14 Valentine

23 Polycarp

March

7 Thomas Aquinas

17 Patrick

21 Benedict

April

14 Justin Martyr

21 Anselm

May

2 Athanasius

4 Monica

June

5 Boniface

9 Columba

July

23 Bridget

* Dates of some observances vary.

August

10 Laurence

13 Hippolytus

13 Radegund

18 Helena

20 Bernard

28 Augustine

September

3 Gregory

25 Sergius

29 Michael and All Angels

30 Jerome

October

4 Francis of Assisi

November

11 Martin

16 Margaret

17 Elizabeth

17 Hilda

22 Cecelia

23 Clement

25 Katherine

December

6 Nicholas

7 Ambrose

20 Ignatius

Bible References

Traditional Symbols

Ambrose: beehive; tower

Anselm: ship; virgin and child

Ansgar: staff tipped with a cross; cross made of stars

Athanasius: open book; equilateral triangle

Augustine: chalice; flaming heart pierced by two arrows

Basil: dove; scroll with words from his writings

Benedict: water flask; briars and roses

Bernard: inkhorn and pen; white dog; beehive

Boniface: ax with fallen oak tree; sword through a Bible

Bridget: pilgrim's staff; lute and chain

Cecelia: harp; two wreaths of roses and lilies

Clement: anchor; fountain

Columba: Celtic cross; white horse

Elizabeth: three crowns; roses in a robe

Francis of Assisi: lighted lamp; birds and animals

Gabriel: scepter and lily; olive branch

Gregory: scroll with music notations; crosier

Helena: hammer and nails; cross of Jerusalem

Hilary: trumpet; pen and three books

Hilda: bird; model of Whitby abbey

Hippolytus: bunch of keys; spear

Ignatius: chains; crucifix

Jerome: open Bible; lion

John Chrysostom: scroll with dove; chalice on Bible

Justin Martyr: soldier's helmet; crossed spears

Katherine: wheel set with sharp knives; sword

Laurence: purse/dish of money; gridiron

Margaret: black cross; scepter and book

Martin: horse; sword cutting a cloak in half

Michael: scales; lance and shield

Monica: IHC on tablet; veil or handkerchief

Nicholas: three joined "pawnbroker" balls; three purses

Patrick: shamrock; snake; Irish harp

Polycarp: dagger; open oven

Radegund: fleur-de-lis symbol; crown and long veil

Raphael: wallet and fish; traveler's staff

Sergius: Russian cross; snowflake

Thomas Aquinas: chalice; stack of books

Uriel: bolt of lightning; scroll with flames

Valentine: heart; sword with sun's rays

Symbols used for saints and angels vary according to place and time in history. Those listed above are only a sample of the many symbolic representations that can be found in Christian artwork and literature through the ages.